A
Gloucestershire
Gallery

A
Gloucestershire
Gallery

edited by
Nigel Scotland

Produced by Sara Shailer
with the support of Cheltenham Tourism

Produced by Sara Shailer with the support of Cheltenham Tourism

First published in 1993 by Nigel Scotland

Copyright © for this collection 1993 Nigel Scotland.
For copyright of individual chapters please refer to the authors of the chapters.

All rights reserved. No part of this publication may be reproduced, stored in a retrieval system, or transmitted in any form or by any means, electronic, mechanical, photocopying, recording, or otherwise, without the prior permission of the publishers and copyright holder.

British Library Cataloguing-in-Publication Data.
A catalogue record for this book is available from the British Library.

ISBN: 0 9522329 0 1

Cover illustrations:

Ralph Richardson as Falstaff (photographed by John Vickers in 1945)
Benjamin Baker (Institution of Civil Engineers)
Edward Wilson (Cheltenham Art Gallery and Museum)

Printed and bound in Great Britain
by Antony Rowe Ltd, Chippenham, Wiltshire

*For the people of Gloucestershire
who have made this book possible*

Contents

	PREFACE	xi
	ACKNOWLEDGEMENTS	xiii
	PICTURE CREDITS	xv
	LIST OF ILLUSTRATIONS	xvii
One	DICK WHITTINGTON *by John Howe*	1
Two	WILLIAM TYNDALE *by Nigel Scotland*	5
Three	KATHERINE PARR *by Brenda Kemeys and Joyce Raggatt*	9
Four	JOHN HOOPER *by Nigel Scotland*	13
Five	HENRY SKILLICORNE *by Steven Blake*	17
Six	ROBERT RAIKES *by Jeremy Whales*	21

A Gloucestershire Gallery

Seven	GEORGE WHITEFIELD *by Nigel Scotland*	25
Eight	WILLIAM BERKELEY *by Steven Blake*	29
Nine	GEORGE ROWE *by Steven Blake*	33
Ten	JOHN KEBLE *by Jeremy Whales*	37
Eleven	FRANCIS CLOSE *by Nigel Scotland*	41
Twelve	FRED ARCHER *by Steven Blake*	45
Thirteen	W.G. GRACE *by Keith Ball*	49
Fourteen	WILLIAM HENLEY *by Cecil Ballantine*	53
Fifteen	JOHN MIDDLETON *by Hugh Greenhalf*	57
Sixteen	ISAAC PITMAN *by Beryl Kingan*	61
Seventeen	DOROTHEA BEALE *by Ann Mentz*	65
Eighteen	BENJAMIN BAKER *by Brian Nottingham*	69
Nineteen	EDWARD WILSON *by Steven Blake*	73
Twenty	JAMES ELROY FLECKER *by Don Hale*	77

Contents

Twenty-One	JOHN NEVIL MASKELYNE *by Michael Seacome*	81
Twenty-Two	ASHTON LISTER *by Charles More*	85
Twenty-Three	GUSTAV HOLST *by Andrew Mulford*	89
Twenty-Four	THE MARTYNS *by John Whitaker*	93
Twenty-Five	IVOR GURNEY *by Anthony Boden*	99
Twenty-Six	GILBERT JESSOP *by Keith Ball*	103
Twenty-Seven	GEORGE DOWTY *by Brian Nottingham*	107
Twenty-Eight	C. DAY LEWIS *by Maurice Bottomley*	111
Twenty-Nine	RALPH RICHARDSON *by Cecil Ballantine*	115
Thirty	ARTHUR TRAVERS HARRIS *by John Rennison*	119

Preface

It has been suggested that the old saying 'as sure as God's Gloucestershire' derived from the fact that Gloucestershire alone of English counties contained four mitred abbeys in the Middle Ages. It may equally be justified by the fact that our county has been the home of many men and women who have distinguished themselves in the service of their fellows. This little book is written in praise of some of them.

Over the years a number of publications on Gloucestershire of varying size and depth have been produced. Most of them are fairly wide-ranging in scope but few of them make much more than a passing reference to any of the remarkable personalities who were born and worked here. It is often rightly said that the story of a place is the story of its people. Part of the aim of this volume is to introduce the reader in a little more detail to the stories of some of those people who have made their mark in the life and work of the county. This is not an exhaustive treatment and there are therefore a number of worthy men and women who have not been included. The approach has been rather to select individuals who distinguished themselves in differing walks of life. These include literature and the arts, scientific discovery, politics and government, the church and the world of sport.

A number of different writers have contributed to this volume. They have been chosen on account of their knowledge and interest in particular individuals. The style of writing is popular rather than scholarly but the details are factually accurate. It is hoped that this book will provide a useful and usable resource for basic information and also at the same time whet the reader's appetite to search for more detailed information concerning the lives of particular individuals that interest them.

Nigel Scotland, Cheltenham, 1993

Acknowledgements

A Gloucestershire Gallery has only been possible through the assistance of the present-day people of Gloucestershire including:

Steven Blake
Stephen Cahill, Photographer
David Clark
Cheltenham Art Gallery and Museum
Cheltenham Tourism
Edward and Sandy Elgar
Everyman Theatre
Gloucester Tourism
Rachel Howls
Louise Kirby
Hilary Quinn
Aylwin Sampson
Dave Shailer
Wotton-under-Edge Historical Society

Picture Credits

The following have kindly granted permission for the inclusion of illustrative material:

Stephen Cahill pp. 2, 3, 24, 46 bottom, 47, 73, 100, 101 top and 101 bottom; Aylwin Sampson pp. 4, 34, 39, 49, 50, 51, 52, 84, 89, 97, 105, 108, 111, 112, 117 and 121; Brenda Kemeys and Joyce Raggatt pp 9 (photographed by kind permission of Kendal Town Council) and 12; Gloucestershire Collection pp. 10, 22, 23, 38, 45 and 55; Cheltenham Art Gallery and Museum pp. 11, 18, 19, 20, 21, 29, 30, 31, 33, 35, 36, 41, 43, 46 top, 57, 58, 74, 76, 90, 91, 92, 104 and 116; The Evangelical Library Ltd p. 25; Hugh Greenhalf p. 59; Mrs Janet Johnstone, Librarian, Cheltenham Ladies' College pp. 66 and 67; Wotton-under-Edge Historical Society pp. 62, 63 and 64; The Institution of Civil Engineers pp. 69 and 70; Railway Magazine p. 71; Dean Close School pp. 77, 78 and 79; David Evans pp. 85, 86 top, 86 bottom, 87 and 88; John Whitaker pp. 94, 95, 96, 98 top and 98 bottom; Anthony Boden p. 99; Brian Nottingham p. 109 (copied by John Cheeseman, Albion Street, Cheltenham); Dowty Group plc p. 110 (copied by Michael Hall Photography, Albion Street, Cheltenham); John Rennison pp. 119 and 120.

We have been unable to trace the precise origin of pictures on pp. 81, 82 and 83. The illustrations were provided by the author of the chapter Michael Seacome who has since sadly died. Despite extensive enquiries, we have also been unable to trace John Vickers to seek permission for the use of the photograph of Ralph Richardson on the front cover and on page 115.

Every effort has been made to trace the owners of illustrations but if any have been inadvertently overlooked please accept our sincere apologies.

List of Illustrations

2	Two effigies in Coberley Church
3	Coberley church from the north
4	The southside of the church showing the doorway in the churchyard wall leading from Coberley Hall, home of Joan and Thomas Berkeley
5	Little Sodbury Manor, Tyndale's home in 1521–1522
6	An early edition of Tyndale's New Testament
7	William Tyndale
8	Katherine Parr's Prayer Book
10	Katherine Parr, a portrait published in 1777
11	The Chapel at Sudeley Castle in 1809
12	Katherine's tomb in Sudeley Castle Chapel
13	John Hooper
14, 15	Extract from Foxe's *Book of Martyrs*
18	Henry Skillicorne
19	The Well Walk in the 1820s
20	Epitaph to Henry Skillicorne in St Mary's Church, Cheltenham
21	Gloucester City in the early eighteenth century
22	The penitentiary in Gloucester in 1795
23	An engraving of Robert Raikes
24	St Mary de Crypt, Gloucester, Raikes' final resting place
25	George Whitefield
26	The Bell Inn, Gloucester, birthplace of George Whitefield
29	Members of the Berkeley Hunt, by Richard Dighton, about 1840
30	William Berkeley, by Richard Dighton, about 1840
31	The Berkeley Hunt's kennels at Cheltenham, about 1825
33	George Rowe's office in Cheltenham
34	George Rowe from a watercolour portrait by his daughter *c.* 1845

A Gloucestershire Gallery

35	A lithographic print of the High Street in Tewkesbury by George Rowe, 1839
36	Part of the 1841 Exhibition of the works of Art and Science at Cheltenham
38	John Keble
39	Keble's birthplace in Fairford
41	Close preaching in the parish church of St Mary's, Cheltenham, about 1838
42	The Very Reverend Francis Close when Dean of Carlisle
43	The Church of England Training College in Swindon Road, Cheltenham
44	Title page of one of Close's sermons
45	Fred Archer's birthplace off St George's Place, Cheltenham
46	Fred Archer
46	The King's Arms in Prestbury today
47	The King's Arms still commemorates its association with Fred Archer with this plaque
49	The Grace Memorial Gates at Lord's
50	W.G. Grace in later years
51	Cheltenham College ground where Grace passed 300 runs in an innings in 1876
52	A cast of Grace's bowling hand
55	William Henley
57	All Saints Church as it would have looked with its completed tower and spire
58	An artist's impression of St Mark's Church, showing the magnificent tower and spire
59	John Middleton
62, 63	Examples of Pitman's 'writing by sound'
64	Advertisement for The Pitman Centenary Commemoration Dinner, 1937
66	Dorothea Beale characteristically holding the flower emblem of the Ladies' College
67	Photograph of girls in the science laboratory at the turn of the century
69	The building of the Forth Bridge
70	Benjamin Baker
71	Benjamin Baker's living model, with Mr Watanabe in the middle
73	The statue of Edward Wilson in the Promenade, Cheltenham
74	Edward Wilson
76	Antarctic watercolour by Edward Wilson
77	James Elroy Flecker
78	James Elroy's father Dr William Flecker, the first headmaster of Dean Close School
79	A family group taken in 1906 on the occasion of the Silver Wedding of Dr and Mrs Flecker

Contents

81	John Nevil Maskelyne
82	Maskelyne's masterpiece Zoe, a young lady who could sketch any celebrity chosen by the audience
83	Maskelyne conducting one of his escape illusions
84	12 Rotunda Terrace, Montpellier, Cheltenham
85	Sir Ashton Lister, knighted by George V in 1911
86	George Lister
86	Some early Lister dairy equipment, 1896.
87	Employees of R.A. Lister and Co. Ltd returning to work after dinner in 1914, photographed in Long Street, Dursley
88	A Lister petrol engine, 1909
89	Holst's birthplace in Clarence Road, now the Holst Birthplace Museum
90	Gustav Holst
91	Bedroom in the Holst Birthplace Museum
92	The 1887 Cheltenham Grammar School
94	H.H. Martyn's own stone carving skills are present in this reredos executed soon after 1888
95	The founder of H.H. Martyn and Co., H.H. Martyn, aged 71 and his wife Fanny (née Clissold)
96	The interior of the *SS Otranto*
97	View of Sunningend factory, Cheltenham
98	Erecting shop in the Sunningend factory, Cheltenham, of H.H. Martyn
98	A.W. Martyn, founder of the Gloster Aircraft Co.
99	Ivor Gurney
100	All Saints' Church, Barton Street, Gloucester
101	Ivor Gurney's grave, Twigworth Parish Church, near Gloucester
104	Gilbert Laird Jessop, by A. Chevallier Tayler, 1905
105	No. 30 Cambray Place, birthplace of Jessop
108	10 Lansdown Terrace Lane, Cheltenham
109	George Dowty beside an undercarriage test bed
110	Arle Court, Cheltenham
111	C. Day Lewis
112	Box Cottage in Bafford Lane, Charlton Kings, Cheltenham
115	Ralph Richardson as Falstaff
116	The Opera House in Cheltenham in about 1900
117	Richardson's birthplace in Tivoli Road, Cheltenham
119	Arthur Travers Harris, Marshal of the RAF
120	The Jolly Roger, a Stirling bomber, with the air and ground crew of 199 Squadron
121	Queen's Parade, Cheltenham, Harris' birthplace in 1892

Chapter One

Dick Whittington

The tale of Dick Whittington and his cat is unique among children's stories in using a real person as its hero. Richard Whittington was Lord Mayor of London in 1397, 1406 and 1419 and his name appears in royal documents at the Public Record Office as well as in City and Guild records. His will was proved in March 1423. The amount of this written evidence is not great, but material evidence about Whittington is even more scanty. His tomb in the church of St Mary de Paternoster in the City of London, and his house near the church must have been destroyed by the Great Fire of London, if not before. Four spoons which he gave to the Mercers' Company and a picture of himself on the manuscript rules of the hospital which he endowed seem to be all that remains.

We do not know where or when Richard Whittington was born. His father, Sir W. Whittington, owned land at Pauntley, near Newent, and married the widow of Thomas Berkeley some time in the 1350s. She continued to hold Berkeley land round Coberley and a local tradition claimed that Richard lived there as a boy, and that two effigies in the church were of his parents. The style of the effigies suggests that this is not so, and there is no documentary evidence to back the story. Richard may have been born in Coberley or in Pauntley, where the family continued to live, or perhaps on another family estate. We do know, however, that he was a younger son so he had little hope of an inheritance and would have had to make his own way in the world. For an ambitious young man the obvious place to go was London.

London was already the largest and richest English city, prospering principally on the wool and cloth trade. The city and its trade were controlled by tightly organized guilds dominated by rich merchants. Since the king often had to borrow money and London was the only place he could do this, the merchants had a hold over the king and won a large measure of self government.

We do not know how Richard left Gloucestershire and arrived in London, how

A Gloucestershire Gallery

Two effigies in Coberley church, traditionally believed to be of Dick Whittington's parents

he became a mercer (cloth-dealer) or succeeded in business. His name appears for the first time in City records in 1379 when he contributed to a City loan. He supplied cloth to the king and other leading families and soon became probably the richest man in London.

Surviving records tell us a little about three aspects of his life. Firstly, he was a leader of the City. He was Lord Mayor three times and had other important jobs including the collection of taxes. He was possibly an MP in 1416. He took his duties seriously: for example, the Brewers' Company records show him trying to keep down prices and check excess profits in the 1420s.

Secondly, Richard lent money to the king and indeed was one of the largest lenders to the crown for over two decades. He was Lord Mayor when Henry IV seized power and kept the City safe in the troubled times. Henry appointed him to the Royal Council, showing the importance of London's support.

Lastly, we know Richard was generous to the City. He paid for repairs and improvements to the Guildhall, Newgate gaol and other buildings, improved water supplies and endowed individual charities including his hospital. It is striking that all his gifts and charities were for London and he seems to have done nothing for his native Gloucestershire. He gave his money away because he had no children and, unlike other successful merchants, did not buy a country estate to

Dick Whittington

Coberley church from the north

house a family. Instead he could found charities which carried his name and keep his memory alive in popular legend.

The legend probably began during his lifetime although the earliest reference to the story is dated 1605 and the earliest surviving version from 1641. Parts of it, as we have seen, are confirmed from other records. As a younger son he must have begun life relatively poor and he did indeed become very rich. He was just as Bow Bells told him 'Thrice Mayor of London'. His wife was Alice Fitzwaryn. She was, however, the daughter of a West Country land owner, not a merchant, and there is no documentary evidence of how they met. Whittington was never knighted so the story of the splendid banquet of the king during which Whittington cancelled the royal debts and received a knighthood cannot be true. Our problem lies in the nature of historical evidence which only covers parts of life. Official records can tell us about royal debts and civic offices but not about where Whittington went to school, how he began in business, how he met his wife

A Gloucestershire Gallery

The southside of the church showing the doorway in the churchyard wall leading from the former Coberley Hall, home of Joan and Thomas Berkeley

or why he was so successful. Nor, alas, can we be sure about the cat. A portrait of 'R Whittington' with his hand on a cat is sadly of a Tudor gentleman and the cat has been added to the picture. The portrait shows the popularity of the story but does not prove it is true. Folk tales of people helped to success by animals are widespread so perhaps this idea was simply added to Whittington's story.

John Howe

Chapter Two

William Tyndale

William Tyndale (1495–1536), translator of the English New Testament, was born in the Slimbridge area of Gloucestershire and came from a family of well-to-do yeoman farmers. He entered Magdalen Hall in Oxford University where the lectures were apparently dull and monotonous. However, in the corridors and narrow streets, the students were almost totally absorbed at the time with the teaching of Martin Luther. John Foxe, the martyrologist, relates that Tyndale made 'great progress in the knowledge of language' and so he went on to Cambridge for further studies.

Little Sodbury Manor, Tyndale's home in 1521–1522

The Gospell

of S. Mathew.

The first Chapter.

This is the boke of the generacion of Jesus Christ the son ne of David, the sonne also of Abraham.

Abraham begat Isaac:
Isaac begat Jacob:
Jacob begat Judas and his brethren:
Judas begat Phares and zaram of Thamar:
Phares begat Hesrom:
Hesrom begat Aram:
Aram begat Aminadab:
Aminadab begat Naasson:
Naasson begat Salmon:
Salmon begat Booz of Rahab:
Booz begat Obed of Ruth:
Obed begat Jesse:
Jesse begat David the kynge:
David the kynge begat Salomon, of her that was the wyfe of Ury:
Salomon begat Roboam:
Roboam begat Abia:
Abia begat Asa:
Asa begat Josaphat:
Josaphat begat Joram:
Joram begat Osias:

David and Abraham are first rehersed: because that Christ was specially promised vnto the, to be of their seede

Genesis. xxviij.g.

i. Parall. ij.a.

Rut.iiij.d

ii. Regū vij.f.
j. Parall. iij.β.

A.H.   Osias

An early edition of Tyndale's New Testament

William Tyndale

William Tyndale

Tyndale began to yearn for peace and quiet to study the scriptures and, in 1521, took up the position of tutor to the children of Sir John Welch at Old Sodbury about ten miles from his family home. According to Foxe, 'there resorted sundry abbots, deans, archdeacons with divers, other doctors and great beneficed men'. Tyndale's knowledge of the scriptures exposed their ignorance much to his employer's delight.

During his spare time, Tyndale preached at various places in the locality including Bristol, a city twice the size of Gloucester with 6,000 inhabitants. He was appalled at the ignorance of the local clergy and it is probably in this context that he uttered his often quoted lines: 'If God spare my life ere many years I will cause a boy that driveth the plough to know more of the scripture than thou dost.' From this point on Tyndale was convinced that he must put the Bible in English into the hands of the English people.

At this time no Bible translation was allowed without the permission of a bishop. William, therefore, tried to secure the patronage of Bishop Tunstall of London. This failed but eventually Geoffrey of Monmouth, a London alderman, financed his trip to Germany in 1524. He visited Luther at Wittenberg and began translating the New Testament into English. By 1527, copies were beginning to flood the English market, much to the displeasure of the church authorities.

In 1525, Cardinal Wolsey, who reigned supreme in church and state, tried unsuccessfully to have Tyndale arrested but he managed to escape to Marburg. Here he printed his *Parable of the Wicked Mammon* which dealt with the central Reformation doctrine of justification by faith. In 1528, Tyndale wrote *The Obedience of the Christian Man* in which he stressed the doctrine of passive obedience to the rulers of the state. Henry VIII was, needless to say, delighted with the book and apparently exclaimed: 'The book is for me and all kings'. His next book *The Practice of Prelates*, however, angered the King as Tyndale came down heavily against Henry's plan to divorce Katherine and marry Anne Boleyn.

In 1531 Henry himself tried to persuade Tyndale to return to England. When he wisely declined, the King demanded his surrender from the Holy Roman Emperor. Eventually in 1535 a young Englishman, Henry Phillips, decoyed him from his house and he was trapped by imperial officers. Thomas Cromwell and a number of English merchants petitioned for his release but to no avail. He was tried and condemned to death for heresy. According to Foxe his last prayer was 'Lord open the King of England's eyes.'

William Tyndale will always be remembered for his translation of the Bible though he did not live to see the task completed. The enduring quality of his work is witnessed by the fact that three-quarters of the King James Version of the New Testament is taken straight from Tyndale's translation.

Nigel Scotland

Chapter Three
Katherine Parr

Katherine Parr (1512–48), the eldest daughter of Sir Thomas and Lady Parr, was born in Kendal in 1512. She was a lady of medium height, with auburn hair, hazel eyes, and a scholastic nature. After the death of her husband, Lady Maud, following the custom of the day, arranged a marriage between Katherine and Edward, son of Sir Thomas Burgh of Old Hall, Gainsborough. Edward did not enjoy good health and died in 1531.

Katherine returned to London to her uncle, Sir William Parr. Two years later she met and married John Neville, Lord Latimer. He was a gentleman-pensioner and an MP for Yorkshire. As Lady Latimer, Katherine took on the role of mother to Latimer's two children, John and Margaret, by a previous marriage. In Katherine these two children found a pious, intelligent woman, a quiet person

Katherine Parr's Prayer Book, which is held in Kendal Town Hall

with gentle wit. She personally undertook their education. Margaret Latimer adored her. In her will Margaret declared 'I am never able to render to her grace sufficient thankes for the godlye education and tender love and bountifull goodnes

A Gloucestershire Gallery

Katherine Parr, a portrait published in 1777

goodnes whiche I have ever more found in her . . .'*. On 2 March 1543, Latimer died, leaving Katherine a wealthy widow.

Following the death of Latimer, Katherine became known to Sir Thomas

* The Complete Peerage, *Volume III, London 1929, section on John (Neville) Lord Latimer*

Katherine Parr

The Chapel at Sudeley Castle in 1809

Seymour, brother of the late Queen Jane. She was attracted to him and the feeling appears to have been mutual. Unfortunately, Henry VIII also noticed Katherine. Once again single, he decided a twice-widowed lady would make an ideal wife. His proposal was one which Katherine, however much she may have wanted to, could not refuse. They were married on 12 July 1543 at Hampton Court.

Life with Henry was precarious. Although she brought the royal children together, and nursed Henry patiently, Katherine had to suppress her interest in the new reformed religion. On one notable occasion she did attempt to debate a point, to distract him from his pain she later explained, and only escaped certain death by staging a superb hysterical outburst.

While married to Henry, Katherine took solace in her books. She began writing her own prayers and meditations against a background of political and religious turmoil. Some of this work is extant and shows the great depth and feeling of her religious views.

A month after Henry's death in 1547, Sir Thomas Seymour was created Baron Seymour of Sudeley by Edward VI. Three months later Katherine and Thomas were secretly married. Princess Elizabeth joined the household and, shortly after Katherine became pregnant, Seymour started to flirt with her. This led to a stormy period, which ended in Elizabeth being sent away. During June 1548 Katherine travelled to Sudeley Castle in Gloucestershire. It was August before Seymour joined his wife to await the birth of their child.

A Gloucestershire Gallery

Katherine's tomb in Sudeley Castle Chapel

Their daughter, Mary, was born on 30 August 1548. On 7 September Katherine died of puerperal fever. Seymour returned to London leaving the young Lady Jane Grey to act as chief mourner at Katherine's funeral. Mary was given into the care of Katherine, Duchess of Suffolk, but she died in infancy.

Even after death Katherine was not allowed to rest in peace. During the Civil War the tomb was desecrated by Parliamentarian troops and her coffin was opened several times, until it was finally laid to rest at Sudeley, in the 1930s, in the tomb we see today, by the members of the Dent family.

Brenda Kemeys and Joyce Raggatt

Chapter Four

John Hooper

John Hooper (*c.* 1495–1555) is remembered as the Protestant martyr Bishop of Gloucester who died in the reign of 'bloody Mary'. His impressive memorial stands close to the spot just outside the west gate to the cathedral precinct. He was burned at the stake at Gloucester on 9 February 1555 for 'the example of others'.

John was a Somerset man who graduated at Oxford in 1519. For most of his early years he was a Cistercian monk at Cleeve Abbey in Somerset and afterwards in Gloucester. When the order was closed down at the Dissolution in 1537, Hooper was the tenth name on the list of 13 monks who were pensioned off.

John Hooper

He went to London where he was converted to the doctrines of the Reformation through the writings of the continental theologians Zwingli and Bullinger. He returned to Oxford to teach the doctrines of Protestantism. After a disagreement with the university authorities, Hooper found a brief period of peace and quiet serving as chaplain and steward in the household of Thomas Arundel. Discovering his opinions, however, his new employer sent him to Bishop Gardiner to convert him back to the catholic faith.

Hooper fled to Europe and in 1546 married Anna de Tserclas at Basle. He spent time in Basle and in Zurich where he established a close friendship with

Foxe's Book of Martyrs

Sir Anthony Kingston, a former friend of the bishop's, had been appointed to attend at his execution. As soon as he saw the bishop he burst into tears. Hooper did not at first recognise him, when Sir Anthony said—

"Why, my lord, do not you know me—an old friend of your's—Anthony Kingston?"

"Yes, Sir Anthony, I do know you well, and am glad to see you in health, and praise God for the same."

"But I am sorry, my lord, to see you in this case, for, as I understand, you are come hither to die. But, alas! consider that life is sweet, and death is bitter; therefore, seeing life may be had, desire to live, for life hereafter may do good."

"Indeed, it is true, Sir Anthony; I am come hither to end this life, and to suffer death here, because I will not gainsay the truth that I have heretofore taught amongst you in this diocese and elsewhere; and I thank you for your friendly counsel, although it be not as I could have wished it."

Sir Anthony then took leave of him, not without shedding bitter tears, and tears also ran down the face of the good bishop. At eight the next morning, the commissioners who were appointed to witness the execution arrived, accompanied by a large band of men. On seeing such a strongly-armed guard, Hooper said, "I am no traitor, neither needed you to have made such a business to bring me to the place where I must suffer; for if you had allowed me, I would have gone alone to the stake, and troubled none of you." Having been strictly forbidden to speak, he went in silence to the appointed place, smiling cheerfully on any whom he knew; he walked with difficulty, as he was suffering much from sciatica, which he had caught in prison. Upwards of 7,000 persons were congregated to see the last scene, the boughs of the trees in the square being used as seats. Three iron hoops had been prepared to fasten him to the stake, and he had three bags of gunpowder tied to him. When he had been secured, he pointed out how the faggots should be placed, and even arranged some with his own hands. There was a strong wind, and the greater part of the faggots being green, it was a long time before they caught fire. Three times were they lighted before they really began to burn up, and even when the gunpowder exploded it did him no good. He was heard to pray aloud, "Lord Jesus, have mercy upon me! Lord

382

Jesus, receive my spirit!" These were the last words he was heard to utter; but when he was black in the mouth, and his tongue so swollen that he could not speak, yet his lips were seen to move. In three quarters of an hour his body fell forwards, and he was released from his sufferings.*

A Gloucestershire Gallery

Heinrich Bullinger, a prominent reforming scholar. He returned to England as soon as Henry VIII died and became chaplain to the Protector, Edward Seymour. Devoting himself to preaching, according to John Foxe, the martyrologist, 'the people in great companies and flocks came daily to hear his voice, and often were unable to get into church on account of the crowd; he used continually to preach, most times twice, at least once, every day.'

In 1550 Hooper was nominated Bishop of Gloucester by the Duke of Northumberland who succeeded Seymour as head of the Regency council. He was very reluctant to become a bishop because he disliked the vestments and oath-taking ceremony. Eventually he complied. After his consecration he developed an unexpected friendship with Northumberland.

As Bishop of Gloucester, Hooper showed himself to be a devoted pastor with a real concern for the poor. Needy local people were often invited into his residence and served a hearty meal. Hooper preached three times a day and did his best to organize his diocese on the Zurich model with superintendents and presbyteries instead of rural deans. He was particularly concerned with the ignorance of many of his clergy. At his visitation of the Gloucester diocese in 1551 he found that of 311 clergy, 10 could not say the Lord's Prayer, 27 did not know who authored it, and 30 did not know where it could be found in the Bible. Hooper also drew up *Fifty-Four Articles* of Protestant teaching for his clergy. In 1552 he resigned the See which was then amalgamated with Worcester. He was appointed the Bishop of Worcester and Gloucester. He administered the new diocese on much the same lines as before but met with greater opposition.

On Mary's accession in 1553, Hooper was one of the first to have proceedings taken against him. The chief charges were that he was married and he did not believe that Jesus was physically present in the Eucharist. He was sent to Gloucester for the execution and burnt on 9 February 1555. In the fire he prayed in a loud voice 'Lord Jesus have mercy upon me, Lord Jesus receive my spirit'.

Nigel Scotland

Previous double page: Extract from Foxe's Book of Martyrs

Chapter Five

Henry Skillicorne

It is a pity that so little is known about Captain Henry Skillicorne (1678–1763), the 'founding father' of the Cheltenham Spa. A Victorian transcription of part of his now-lost diary and his lengthy memorial tablet in Cheltenham's St Mary's Church are virtually the only sources for his life.

A Manxman by birth, Skillicorne had a colourful career as a seaman, for many years in the service of a leading Bristol merchant, Jacob Elton. Skillicorne eventually settled in Bristol, and it was there, in 1731, that he married Elizabeth Mason, the daughter of the late William Mason of Cheltenham.

Skillicorne's marriage was to have a profound effect upon both his own future, and that of the small market town of Cheltenham. Among Mason's property at Cheltenham was the field on the slopes of Bays Hill, to the south of the town, in which rose the mineral spring on which Cheltenham's future as a spa was to be based. That spring had been discovered in about 1716, and already Mason had gone some way towards its exploitation by enclosing it, building a thatched shed above it, and charging for its use. But it needed the experience and foresight of such a man as Skillicorne to turn the embryonic spa into something of more than local significance. That is precisely what he did following his and Elizabeth's move from Bristol to Cheltenham in 1738.

Finding the spring open and exposed to the weather, he built a brick canopy above it large enough to accommodate several 'drinkers' and the 'pumper', who was employed to serve the former with their glasses of Cheltenham's briny-tasting beverage. The spring itself was deepened, a pump was installed, and a small 'assembly room' was built to one side, where visitors could meet, play billiards and cards, and attend the balls and public breakfasts that were an essential part of life at any spa. To link his new spa buildings to the town, and no doubt to create a landscape feature reminiscent of Bath or the Bristol Hotwell, Skillicorne planted a tree-lined 'walk' of elms and limes between the well and the small River Chelt.

Henry Skillicorne

From there, a wooden bridge led to a path across Church Meadow (now the site of Royal Crescent) to the parish church and High Street. A second avenue of trees was planted to the south of the well. These tree-lined paths soon became known as the Well Walk, and were to be the basis of one of Cheltenham's most characteristic urban forms, the leafy avenue, as it grew as a spa town over the next century.

The Well Walk in the 1820s

Skillicorne's success, at least in the short term, may be measured from the extracts from his diary that are included in John Goding's *History of Cheltenham*, first published in 1853. The various improvements at the spa were undertaken between 1739 and 1742, and in each year the number of visitors (or subscribers as they were usually known, as each had to 'subscribe' by paying a fee to drink there), was considerable, peaking at 674 in 1741 and averaging 571 each year between then and 1747.

Unfortunately, this period of unprecedented success did not last. It is clear that the spa was less successful in the 1750s and '60s, hindered perhaps by a lack of accommodation at Cheltenham and the difficult journey to and from the town.

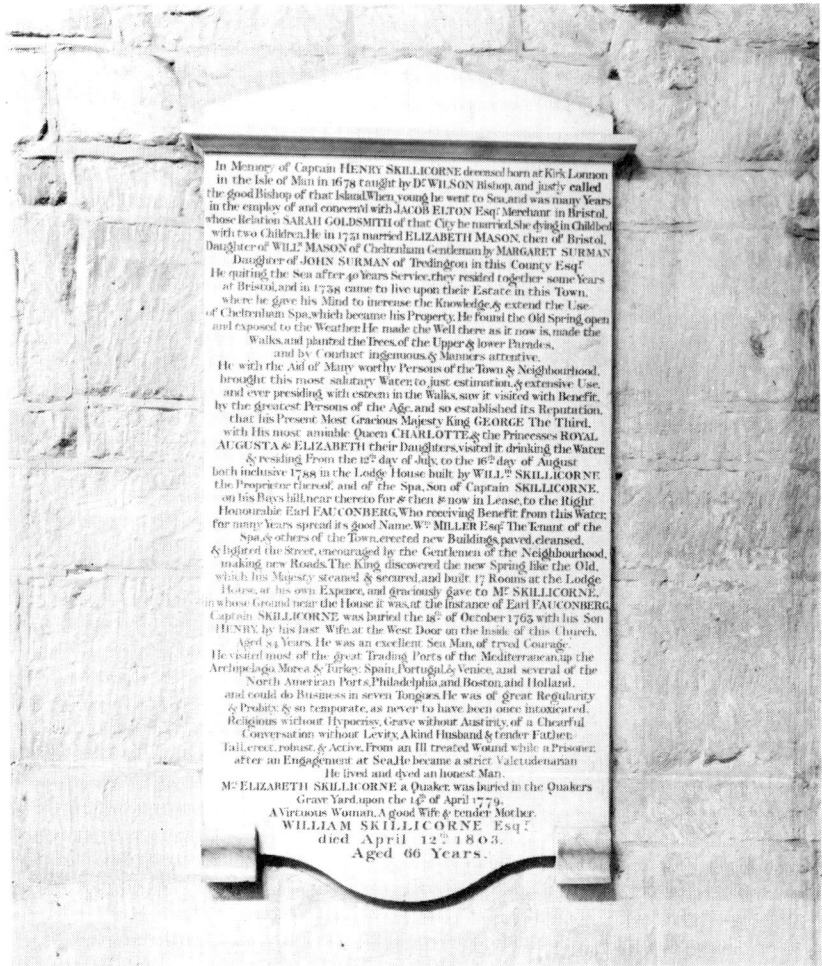

Epitaph to Henry Skillicorne in St Mary's Church, Cheltenham

Skillicorne cannot therefore have been a totally happy man as he lived out his old age in Cheltenham, where he died in October 1763. He certainly could not have predicted the dramatic revival that was to take place during the coming years, nor that his son William, who took over the running of the well, would be able to count the King and Queen among his visitors just a quarter of a century later.

Steven Blake

Chapter Six

Robert Raikes

Robert Raikes was born in Gloucester on 14 September 1735, brought up in a large family and educated at the Cathedral school. He was apprenticed to his father who had founded the *Gloucester Journal* in 1722, succeeding to the business on his father's death in 1767.

Young Raikes, a shrewd, industrious businessman, 'cut a dash' in the City of Gloucester. An ardent churchman, he was nonetheless stylish, elaborate and conspicuous, leading his detractors to think him vain and self-centred.

He built on the *Journal*'s popularity, moved the printing office, and then changed the day of publication. This meant editorial work on a Sunday and led to

Gloucester City in the early eighteenth century

A Gloucestershire Gallery

The penitentiary in Gloucester in 1795

the legendary incident which was to make him a figure of national importance. As he sat at his desk one Sunday, a stone crashed through the windows above his head. Looking up, he was in time to see a gang of young ruffians escaping down the road. Sunday, a day of rest, was the most noisy and violent day of the week in Gloucester, and this incident angered and disturbed him.

Later, as he paid one of his regular visits to the gaol, he reflected, as he walked, on the tragedy of so many young lives maimed before they had a chance to grow. He stopped momentarily and asked himself whether anything could be done. An inner voice answered 'Try', and as he explained in old age, 'I did try, and see what God has wrought'. Where the clergy had failed, Raikes succeeded. In Gloucester gaol, he initiated a simple, effective scheme of reading and religious education in which the quick, able scholars taught the beginners.

Raikes joined forces with Thomas Stock, a local curate, who had pioneered a Sunday School in his parish. Using his own money and resources, and with crusading zeal, Raikes found premises, selected teachers, and drew up basic rules. He then set out to recruit children from the 'very poorest, ragged, hard-swearing and ill disciplined homes'. He visited each home personally, and encouraged parental co-operation.

The early days were fraught with difficulty, the children 'turrible chaps, with bad 'uns coming in'; wild animals were let loose in the classes, and fights were frequent. Yet Raikes and his teachers persevered and, in time, succeeded. He insisted that the children arrive at school with clean hands, clean faces, and hair combed. He bought books and materials, was generous with treats and prizes for courtesy and achievement, and won the children's confidence and respect. His own enthusiasm was infectious. On one occasion, following his demonstration of the drawing power of the magnet, and likening it to the power of Jesus to attract disciples, his band of 'ragged missionaries' arrived at the Cathedral for the 7 a.m. service the next Sunday with a great crowd of new recruits for his school!

An engraving of Robert Raikes

The social effect of the Sunday Schools was impressive. The day of violence became the day of tranquillity. After three years Raikes published the work of the schools in his *Journal* and, to his astonishment, within months the success of his scheme had reached all parts of the British Isles.

Many influential people now became involved in the work, and visitors from all parts of the country came to Gloucester for advice. The success of his achievement was publically acknowledged when he was invited by Queen Victoria to Windsor Castle.

At a time of great social upheaval, dreadful poverty, harsh penal laws and starvation in the county, Raikes proved to a querulous public the 'civilising influence' of his Sunday Schools.

Once held up at pistol point by a highwayman on a journey to London, Raikes believed firmly in the maintenance of law and order, yet such compassion for the poor and the needy flowed from his pen as to touch the hearts of his readers and enlist their support for the causes he espoused.

Generous to his friends, hospitable to his many visitors, a caring husband and father, Raikes was also a man of considerable personal courage. He braved riots in the streets and disease in prison to effect his work. Only in his inability to give due credit to those who shared his vision and his work is he to be faulted.

He retired from the *Journal* in 1802, continuing his interest in the work of the Cathedral and parish church, St Mary de Crypt, his final resting place. He died on

A Gloucestershire Gallery

St Mary de Crypt, Gloucester, Raikes' final resting place

5 April 1811 and is commemorated by a statue on the London Embankment.

More importantly, his memory is inscribed in the minds of those who believe that Education is the key to a better and more compassionate society.

Jeremy Whales

Chapter Seven

George Whitefield

George Whitefield (1714–70), the Methodist evangelist, was born at the Bell Inn in Gloucester which was kept by his father. He attended the Crypt school in the city but had little liking for learning. After a brief spell away working for his father, George went back to the school and then in 1732 gained entry into Pembroke College, Oxford, as a servitor. He was attracted by the Oxford Methodists and ordered his life by their strict patterns of behaviour. In Easter 1735 he underwent an experience which he described as 'a new birth'.

In 1736 he graduated with a BA and became leader of the few Methodists who remained in Oxford after John and Charles Wesley had left to work in America. Despite being only 21 years of age instead of the required 23, George was ordained deacon by Bishop Benson of Gloucester. Hearing that his first sermon had driven 15 people mad, the bishop said he hoped they wouldn't recover in time for another dose the following week! Whitefield undoubtedly possessed extra-ordinary powers as a preacher.

In March 1738 Whitefield made a brief visit to Georgia, arriving at Savannah in May and returning to London in November. In January 1739 he was 'priested' at

George Whitefield

A Gloucestershire Gallery

The Bell Inn, Gloucester, birthplace of George Whitefield

Oxford and preached to a large congregation in St Alban's church. The following month he journeyed to Bristol with the aim of preaching to raise money for an orphan house in Georgia. Finding the town's clergy unsympathetic and their churches closed to him, Whitefield preached in the open air at Kingswood in April where he recorded that at 'a moderate computation there were about ten thousand people to hear me'. He went on into Gloucestershire preaching to 600 in fields belonging to an inn in Stroud, and to 3,000 in Gloucester Cathedral on Sunday 15 April. The following day he found the inhabitants of Cheltenham 'alarmed' and generally unresponsive. Later the same month he preached to 'an exceeding great multitude at Moorfields' and at Kennington Common where 'no less than thirty thousand people' were supposed to have been present. At these services Whitefield made collections for the orphanage in Georgia which he had founded in January 1740. He travelled extensively, gave up wearing the surplice, exchanged pulpits with the dissenters and disregarded a sentence of suspension passed on him by the church at Charleston.

Whitefield returned to England from a further journey to America in 1741 and championed the cause of predestination against John Wesley. The rift between Whitefield and Wesley was, however, short-lived. Whitefield wrote to Wesley, 'May God remove all obstacles that now prevent our union.'

In 1741 he married Elizabeth James, a widow ten years his senior, whom he described as 'neither beautiful nor rich'. He was elected moderator of the Welsh Calvinists in 1743 and the following year came into contact with Lady Huntingdon, a woman of royal descent. He became her chaplain and she supported his preaching and ministerial activities.

Whitefield is remembered as a gifted and natural preacher. He was a warm-hearted man, eloquent in speech and unsurpassed in dramatic power. The effect of his sermons was extraordinary, producing not only fainting, convulsions and violent agonies among his hearers but also lasting results. He visited America seven times and effected a great revival of religion there. He is said to have preached 18,000 sermons. He died, utterly worn out, on 30 September 1770 and was buried at Newburyport in New Hampshire.

Nigel Scotland

A Gloucestershire Gallery

CIRENCESTER AND GLOUCESTER

Wednesday, June 27. Waited on the minister of the parish, and asked him for the use of his pulpit; but he refused it, because I had not my letters of orders. Went to public worship at eleven; and preached to about three thousand people, in a field near the town, about twelve. Was afterwards visited by several of the Baptist congregation, who brought me five guineas for the Orphan House. Set out about four in the afternoon, and reached Gloucester about seven in the evening, to the inexpressible joy of many. The late report of my being dead has only served to make my present visits more welcome. Thus all things work together for good to those that love God. Soon after I came into the town, I visited the Society, and expounded for the space of an hour to more people than the room (though it was large) would contain. Blessed be God all heard the Word most gladly. I now see the seed sown when I was here last, was not all sown on stony, thorny ground; no, some has been received into honest and good hearts. This is the Lord's doing; to Him be all the glory through Jesus Christ.

GLOUCESTER

Thursday, June 28. Preached in the morning to about a thousand people in my brother's field. Went to public prayers at the Cathedral. Waited upon the Bishop, who received me very civilly. Visited some sick persons in the afternoon who sent for me. Preached at night to upwards of three thousand. Great numbers were melted into tears; and most, I believe, went convicted away. Thanks be to God Who thus giveth us the victory through our Lord Jesus Christ.

GLOUCESTER AND PAINSWICK

Friday, June 29. Preached in my brother's field in the morning to a large and very affected congregation. Went to the Cathedral service. Visited some religious friends; and preached to above three thousand souls in the street at Painswick. All was hushed and silent. The Divine Presence was amongst us. All rejoiced to see me alive again, and thanked God abundantly on my behalf.

Extract from George Whitefield's journal

Chapter Eight

William Berkeley

In many ways, Colonel William Fitzhardinge Berkeley (1786–1857) epitomizes the free-living Regency gentleman, a man whose influence on the life and society of the spa town of Cheltenham was considerable during its fashionable heyday. In addition, the later reformation in his moral behaviour may almost be viewed as paralleling the changes being wrought in society generally, and particularly in the transformation of Cheltenham into a bastion of the Evangelical movement.

Members of the Berkeley Hunt, by Richard Dighton, about 1840

A Gloucestershire Gallery

William Berkeley, by Richard Dighton, about 1840

William was the eldest, illigitimate, son of the 5th Earl of Berkeley and a butcher's daughter, Mary Cole, whom the Earl eventually married in 1796. Known generally as 'the Colonel', he gathered around him both at Berkeley Castle and in Cheltenham a large following of like-minded men and women, who shared his enthusiasm for hunting, racing and the theatre.

In each of these, the Colonel encouraged development. The Berkeley Hunt was one of the county's leading hunts, with its stables in Cheltenham. The

Cheltenham races benefited considerably from his patronage, and he was largely responsible for the first three-day event, on Cleeve Hill in 1819, and for financially supporting the races over many years, as well as mapping out its first steeplechase course 15 years later. The theatre, which was at its peak in Cheltenham during the early decades of the nineteenth century, earned his particular attention, and

The Berkeley Hunt's kennels at Cheltenham, about 1825

both he and his brothers appeared, as actors, at the town's Theatre Royal.

Inevitably, the Colonel came into conflict with the new Evangelical mood in Cheltenham, which was apparent from the late 1820s. The spa's social heyday had passed and he was often criticized by the forceful incumbent of Cheltenham, the Revd Francis Close. Gradually, however, the Colonel's own lifestyle and attitudes began to change. In 1831, he was elevated to the peerage, as Baron Segrave, and his mind turned more to politics than to pleasure, as a supporter, both financially and practically, of the Liberals. In 1835, he was appointed Lord Lieutenant of Gloucestershire, and in 1841 became Earl Fitzhardinge. Although criticized for maintaining mistresses in Cheltenham, a growing spirituality entered his life. He developed a link with the Congregational church in the town, whose minister, the Revd Andrew Morton Brown, became his spiritual guide, and was summoned to the Earl's bedside in October 1857, shortly before he died from the effects of a riding accident a few months before.

Steven Blake

Chapter Nine

George Rowe

Although George Rowe (1795–1864) was a native of Devonshire, he spent 20 years, between 1832 and 1852, living and working in Cheltenham. He played a major role in the life of the town as well as consolidating his position as one of the leading topographical printmakers of his day.

Rowe, the son of an Exeter builder, showed considerable artistic talent from an early age and made a career for himself as a drawing master, first at Exeter and then at Hastings. While at Hastings, in the 1820s, he added a further dimension to his career by preparing views of the town and its surroundings for publication by a local librarian as souvenirs for visitors to the area. The technique that Rowe used to produce the prints, that of lithography (in which the prints were made from a prepared stone, on which the image had been drawn in reverse), enabled them to be produced in far larger numbers than more traditional methods of printing, such as engraving or etching, would allow. This served to reduce the price and therefore to increase their popularity.

George Rowe's office in Cheltenham, from Rowe's Illustrated Cheltenham Guide *(1845)*

Rowe continued to produce topographical prints, as both artist and publisher, after his return to Exeter in 1828, and later at Cheltenham where, by 1836, he had

George Rowe from a watercolour portrait by his daughter c. 1845

established a lithographic printing business of his own. During his career, he produced hundreds of different views, and these are as popular with collectors now as they were when first produced 150 years ago.

During his 20 years in Cheltenham, Rowe became involved in many aspects of the town's life. At one time or another, he was the co-proprietor of one of its newspapers, and of one of its spa wells, an overseer of the poor, a churchwarden, a founder member of the Cheltenham Liberal Association and a member of the Town Commissioners, the forerunner of the present Borough Council. In 1846–7, he occupied the position of High Bailiff of Cheltenham, equivalent to the present position of Mayor.

Sadly, despite all Rowe's business and professional involvements, he failed to prosper, and one of the most remarkable facets of his career is his decision, in 1852, to emigrate to Australia to try his luck at the goldfields, despite being

George Rowe

A lithographic print of the High Street in Tewkesbury by George Rowe, 1839

almost 60 years of age. More remarkable still is the fact that after being forced by ill health to abandon his attempts at prospecting, he found unexpected success once again as an artist, painting and selling portraits of the settlers and views of the goldfields. During his six years in Australia, he proved as prolific an artist as he had in England in previous decades. Following his return to England in 1858, he spent several years preparing a great series of canvasses showing Australian scenes, which won him a medal at the 1862 International Exhibition in London, and which served to establish Rowe as one of Australia's leading goldfields artists, a position that he still retains in Australian art history.

Steven Blake

A Gloucestershire Gallery

Part of the 1841 Exhibition of the works of Art and Science at Cheltenham; Rowe is seen at work in the far right-hand corner producing this very print

Chapter Ten

John Keble

John Keble was born on 25 April 1792 at his family home in Fairford, Gloucestershire. He was educated with his brother Tom by their father, Vicar of Coln St Aldwyns. At the age of 14, he gained a scholarship to Corpus Christi College, Oxford, and four years later won a double first in Classics and Mathematics. Elected to a Fellowship at Oriel College, the most prestigious in the university, he went on to win two major university prizes, and became an Examiner.

A sensitive and devout young man, he spent months in spiritual preparation before being ordained deacon in 1815 by the Bishop of Oxford. Glad to assist his father, he undertook the pastoral care of two small villages, Eastleach and Burthorpe, to which Southrop was added much later.

When he was appointed tutor at Oriel College in 1817, this shy homely don with a playful sense of humour exercised a degree of academic rigour and pastoral care, unusual in his day. His students quickly warmed to him, then revered him. All hoped to be invited to share the long vacations with him at Southrop.

Many of Keble's friends urged him to stand for the provostship of Oriel when it fell vacant in 1827, but John Henry Newman, who considered him 'the first man in Oxford' expressed a more perceptive counsel: 'If an angel's place was vacant, we should look to Keble, but we are only electing a provost.' Keble withdrew.

In that same year, encouraged by his father, and rather against his own judgment, Keble anonymously published *The Christian Year*. To the surprise of his friends, and the embarrassment of William Wordsworth to whom it was dedicated, the poems proved an outstanding success, for quite unconsciously John Keble had caught and interpreted the spirit of the new Romantic age. The poems, dignified, reflective, redolent of Christian antiquity, went through scores of editions, and in time graced the bookshelves of every respectable home in Victorian England.

John Keble

Not surprisingly, Keble was elected Professor of Poetry in 1831, a post which he held for ten years.

At a critical time in Church–State relations, Keble, a tough Tory opposed to Liberalism in any form, made his mark. His Assize sermon in July 1833 signalled the beginning of the Oxford Movement (1833–45). Newman provided the

John Keble

Keble's birthplace in Fairford

inspiration and Keble the guidance in a movement now regarded as having changed the face of English religious life.

Never a man to be hurried, Keble married Charlotte Clarke, a childhood friend, at the age of 43, and embarked on a happy though childless marriage. In the following year he became Vicar of Hursley, Hampshire, a 'nineteenth century time warp' where he remained for 30 years, campaigning vigorously in defence of the church he loved, repudiating Biblical critics as 'too wicked to be reasoned with' and corresponding with a host of friends at home and abroad. He encouraged the saying of the Daily Offices in church, the practice of Confession, and frequent celebrations of Holy Communion. Considered a severe man by his parishioners, he cuffed the insolent and warned the lax, but provided help for the poor in times of distress, and rebuilt the village church and school. The devotional piety and ethical strength of the catholic tradition in the Anglican church is enshrined in Keble's life. His influence was to be found most powerfully at work in the lives of his students and friends, the most notable of whom, in Gloucestershire, was Sir George Prevost, for 59 years Vicar of Stinchcombe. In such men, Keble's pastoral ideals, spirituality and devotion to duty are seen at their best. He was instrumental in the building of Oakridge church, and in assisting the restoration of Bisley and Stinchcombe parish churches.

John Keble died at Bournemouth on 29 March 1866. His rural flock were astonished at 'the wondrous multitude of men and women who came from all parts of the country' to his funeral at Hursley on 6 April, a testimonial to his self-effacing modesty.

Commemorated by a bust in Westminster Abbey, elevated to become an Alternative Saint in the Anglican calendar, his most powerful memorial is in the living stream of men and women educated in the university he loved, and nurtured in the college at Oxford, opened in 1870, which bears his name.

Jeremy Whales

New Every Morning

New every morning is the love
our wakening and uprising prove;
through sleep and darkness safely brought,
restored to life and power and thought.

New mercies, each returning day,
hover around us while we pray;
new perils past, new sins forgiven,
new thoughts of God, new hopes of heaven.

If on our daily course our mind
be set to hallow all we find,
new treasures still, of countless price,
God will provide for sacrifice.

Old friends, old scenes, will lovelier be,
As more of Heaven in each we see:
Some softening gleam of love and prayer
shall dawn on every cross and care.

The trivial round, the common task,
will furnish all we need to ask;
room to deny ourselves; a road
to bring us daily nearer God.

Only, O Lord, in Thy dear love
fit us for perfect rest above;
and help us, this and every day,
to live more nearly as we pray.

Chapter Eleven

Francis Close

Francis Close (1797–1882) was the redoubtable incumbent of Cheltenham during the middle years of the nineteenth century. He achieved notoriety for a number of reasons including his denunciation of the town's race- and theatre-goers, his tirades against the Chartists and Owenite radicals and his continuous fulmination against the growing ritualist trends in the Church of England. For this and much more, the poet Tennyson dubbed him 'the Pope of Cheltenham'.

Francis was born in Frome, Somerset, the fourth and youngest son of the Revd Henry Jackson Close. He was educated at Merchant Taylors' School and St John's

Close preaching in the parish church of St Mary's, Cheltenham, about 1838

The Very Reverend Francis Close when Dean of Carlisle

College, Cambridge where he showed little inclination for mathematics and a real taste for boating. He left university with only an ordinary degree but with strong evangelical convictions. The same year he married Anna Diana Arden. They were to have four sons and four daughters.

Ordained in 1821, Close became incumbent of Cheltenham parish church in 1826. He was directly responsible for building four new churches in the town, St Paul's in 1831, Christ Church in 1840, St Peter's in 1849 and St Luke's in 1854. All the clergy who served these places of worship were Close's nominees, men who were ready to side with him in his campaign against the local Roman Catholic community. According to contemporary reports his annual anti-papal diatribes stirred the Protestants to fever pitch on Guy Fawkes day.

It was as an educationalist that Close really qualifies as a minor national figure. In his early years he was a strong supporter of the National Society which built

Francis Close

The Church of England Training College in Swindon Road, Cheltenham

infant and day schools in conjunction with the Church of England. Close was responsible for the building of more than a dozen such schools in Cheltenham. Later, however, he fell foul of the National Society when he found it had been taken over by High Churchmen. Close was concerned himself with the education of the middle classes. He overhauled the town's tudor grammar school and helped found Cheltenham College which took its first pupils in 1841.

Against a background of growing Romeward trends, Francis became increasingly determined to train teachers who would have definite Protestant convictions. In 1849 the foundation stone of his new training college in Swindon Road was laid. It was reckoned to be his most significant enterprise.

Close had a lasting distaste for radical politics and preached against the Cheltenham Chartists when they attended morning service as a body in his church. Perhaps no area of Cheltenham was more markedly affected by Close than the town's social life. He lambasted the race-goers in a sermon entitled 'The Evil Consequences of Attending the Race Course'. He attacked the stage which in all ages, he claimed, 'has proved itself to be a matter of immorality and vice'. Close campaigned against Sunday trading and his personal efforts delayed the coming of the railway to Cheltenham for six years. 'Why', he declared, 'should we have the bubbling, hissing roaring, bellowing monster coming within a few yards of our parish church and interrupting our devotion?'.

So supreme was Close in his empire that his opponents nicknamed the spa 'the Close Borough' and his 30-year clerical rule as a 'Close season'.

Nigel Scotland

A Gloucestershire Gallery

THE CHARTISTS' VISIT TO THE PARISH CHURCH.

A SERMON,

ADDRESSED TO THE

CHARTISTS OF CHELTENHAM,

Sunday, August 18th, 1839,

ON THE OCCASION OF THEIR ATTENDING THE PARISH CHURCH IN A BODY.

BY THE

REV F. CLOSE, A. M.
PERPETUAL CURATE.

"MY SON, FEAR THOU THE LORD AND THE KING: AND MEDDLE NOT WITH THEM THAT ARE GIVEN TO CHANGE: FOR THEIR CALAMITY SHALL RISE SUDDENLY; AND WHO KNOWETH THE RUIN OF THEM BOTH?" *Prov.* xxiv. 21, 22.

Twenty-seventh Thousand.

LONDON:
PUBLISHED BY HAMILTON, ADAMS, AND CO.
SOLD ALSO BY
L. & G. SEELEY; J. HATCHARD & SON; & J. NISBET & CO.
1840.
Price Twopence.

Chapter Twelve

Fred Archer

Fred Archer (1857–86), the Cheltenham-born champion jockey, may well be described as England's first 'sporting hero'. He was a man who, in his short and spectacular career, commanded the popular adulation reserved nowadays for film stars and pop singers, as well as earning the patronage of royalty and the aristocracy.

Born in a small cottage off Cheltenham's St George's Place, Archer was the son of William Archer, a steeplechase rider who won the Grand National in 1858, shortly before giving up racing in order to succeed his father-in-law as landlord of the King's Arms public house at Prestbury. William Archer taught his son horsemanship from an early age, and then, perhaps perceiving his son's remarkable talent, apprenticed him to the leading horse-trainer of his day, Mathew Dawson of Newmarket.

Archer made his home at Newmarket from 1868 until his tragic suicide just 18 years later. It was as

Fred Archer's birthplace off St George's Place, Cheltenham

A Gloucestershire Gallery

Fred Archer

one of Dawson's riders that he made his first public appearance 'on the flat', at Newmarket, in October 1869. Despite coming last, he made up for this a month later with his first winner, and winning became the name of the game for Archer thereafter. His natural talent, combined with single-minded training and a ruthless determination to win at all costs, ensured that his catalogue of success steadily increased. In 1874, with 147 wins, he became champion jockey of England, a position that he retained for the rest of his life. In all, he rode 2,148 winners in just 17 years, an achievement that has still not been equalled.

The King's Arms in Prestbury today

Fred Archer

As Archer's success on the racecourse increased, so too did the pressures on his life. Unusually tall for a jockey, at 5 ft 8 1/2 in, Archer had to struggle to keep his weight down, and resorted eventually to a diet of oranges, sardines and champagne, along with frequent turkish baths and purges. His phenomenal record could only be maintained by constant travelling from course to course, and during the latter part of his career he was given no peace by the crowds, who besieged railway stations and hotels to catch a glimpse of him. Media coverage was intense, and by no means always favourable, as accusations of 'race fixing' began to circulate. The cost of building a large house at Newmarket, the demands of his family in Gloucestershire, and his own heavy betting must have drained him further, and the peace that he might have gained from a happy private life also eluded him. In 1883, he married Dawson's daughter, but less than two years

The King's Arms still commemorates its association with Fred Archer with this plaque

later, both she and their first born son were dead, leaving him with an infant daughter to care for.

It was as if misfortune drove Archer on to superhuman feats. A week after his wife's death, he embarked on a four-month tour of America, and during 1885, he rode 246 winners, his highest total ever. The autumn of 1886 saw him dashing from Dublin to Newmarket to Brighton, as his health began to give way and symptoms of a severe chill, later diagnosed as typhoid fever, began to appear. Returning to Newmarket on 4 November 1886, after a series of failures on the courses at Brighton and Lewes, Archer took to his bed and became increasingly depressed and confused; four days later, he took the revolver that he kept beside his bed for fear of burglars, and shot himself through the mouth, killing himself instantly. It was a tragic end to one of the most brilliant careers in the history of horse-racing.

Steven Blake

Chapter Thirteen

W.G. Grace

William Gilbert Grace ('Gibby' to his family) was Gloucestershire's cricket captain from 1871 to 1898. He was a cricketer of unchallenged supremacy whose name lives on in history as the man who made cricket England's national game.

Everyone has heard of him. We can all visualize his huge frame, black, bushy beard which was part of the English landscape for 40 years, over-developed waistline encircled with the MCC tie, brown shoes, under-sized cap balanced precariously on his head, no batting gloves and pads which encased his legs with difficulty. Despite his girth, he possessed remarkable stamina, energy and exceptional skills, having scored almost 55,000 runs including 126 centuries, taken 2,876 wickets, held 877 catches and captained England in 13 Test Matches.

W.G. was born at Downend House near Bristol in 1848 into a family of keen cricketers. His father, Doctor H.M. Grace, made a pitch in front of

The Grace Memorial Gates at Lord's

A Gloucestershire Gallery

W.G. Grace in later years

Cheltenham College ground where Grace passed 300 runs in an innings in 1876

the house and his mother Martha is the only woman to have her birth and death recorded in *Wisden*. He recalled holding a bat when he was two years old, the year that the family moved to a larger house, 'The Chestnuts' also in Downend, where they again made a pitch and his Uncle Pocock, four brothers, four sisters and three dogs (fielders) played continuously.

His first good score was 32 against a strong All England XI on the Downs in Bristol when he was 14 and in the next year he made his first century (170) for South Wales against the Gentlemen of Sussex. Two years later playing for the England XI at the Oval he made 224 not out. Twice in 1876, at Canterbury for the MCC and at Cheltenham for Gloucestershire, he passed 300 runs in an innings. His last century in first-class cricket was on his 56th birthday when he scored 166 against the MCC at the Oval. He played his last game when he was 65 scoring 69 not out.

Stories about W.G. as a person abound. He had a reputation for cunning, arrogance and selfishness in the field, being quite capable of shouting 'Miss it' to a fielder when he was batting, and talking furiously when fielding to disturb the batsman's concentration. He often disputed umpires' decisions and his dictum

A Gloucestershire Gallery

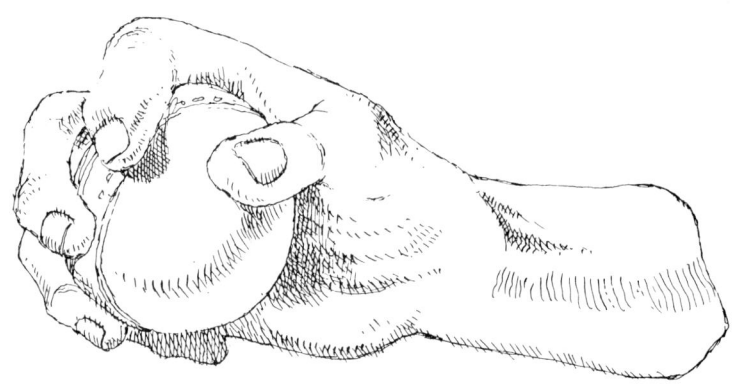

A cast of Grace's bowling hand

was 'get at the bowler before the bowler gets you'. He also made a large amount of money from cricket while always classed as an amateur. Today, we recall all this as 'genial rascality' and prefer to look at his good points, which were many, and included his concern for the poor patients in his working-class medical practice and his kindness to the cricketing professionals who earned little.

Known as 'The Old Man', 'The Doctor' and 'The Champion', W.G. Grace will always be synonymous with cricket. He supposedly had a small, high-pitched voice but everything else about him was big: size of scores, centuries, wickets, physique, length of career (44 seasons) and overbearing presence. His friends adored him and he was universally liked. Although he quarrelled with the committee and walked out on the Gloucestershire Club in 1899, leaving to manage the new London Club at Crystal Palace, he still had the greatest affection for the county of his birth and the row was eventually forgotten.

Grace died in London in 1915 at the age of 67, two weeks after suffering a stroke. There was more to him than exceptional athletic talent, he had an unmistakable personality and charisma which made him a great sporting hero.

Keith Ball

Chapter Fourteen

William Henley

William Ernest Henley was born on 23 August 1849 in Gloucester at 2 Eastgate Street in a house that has since been rebuilt. His father, Ernest Henley, was a bookseller and his mother, Emma Morgan, was descended from Joseph Warton, the seventeenth-century literary critic. Henley was educated at the Crypt School, Gloucester where between 1861 and 1863 the headmaster was the Manx poet, T.E. Brown. He was an important influence on the young Henley and encouraged his interest in literature and the arts.

Although Henley spent his childhood in Gloucester the city features hardly at all in his work. Only in 'The Arabian Nights' Entertainment', written in 1897, does he present any memories of his early environment.

>   . . . the child eyes
> Spelled out the wizard message by the light
>   Of the sober, workaday hours
> They saw, week in week out, pass, and still pass
>   In the sleepy Minster City, folded kind
>   In ancient Severn's arm,
>   Amongst her water-meadows and her docks,
>   whose floating populace of ships –
>   Galliots and luggers, light-heeled brigantines,
>   Bluff barques and rake-hell fore-and-afters –
>   brought
>   To her very doorsteps and geraniums
>   The scents of the World's End; the calls
>   That may not be gainsaid to rise and ride
>   Like fire on some high errand of the race;
>   The irritable appeals

> For comradeship that sound
> Steadily from the irresistible sea.

From the age of 12 Henley became increasingly crippled by tuberculosis which disabled him physically and resulted in the amputation of a foot. In 1873 he was warned that his life could be saved only by the amputation of a leg. He went to Edinburgh to place himself into the hands of Professor Joseph (later Lord) Lister where he remained a patient for 20 months. In the event Lister saved his leg and, although dogged throughout his life by serious illnesses, he was able to pursue a noted career in literary journalism.

While in hospital in Edinburgh he wrote a remarkable series of poems entitled 'In Hospital' which catalogued his experiences. They are not only a moving illustration of Victorian hospital conditions and medical attitudes but they also show Henley's skill at versification. Because of their unconventional, unrhymed form they were rejected by *The Cornhill Magazine* at the time but were later published in 1888.

On leaving the Edinburgh infirmary in 1875 Henley pursued a career as editor of a range of literary journals where he commissioned contributions from many well-known writers. Among them were J.M. Barrie, T.E. Brown (his old headmaster), Thomas Hardy, Rudyard Kipling, R.L. Stevenson, H.G. Wells and W.B. Yeats. He had established a long but not untroubled relationship with Stevenson when in hospital in Edinburgh and portrayed him in one of the hospital poems, 'Apparitions'. He collaborated with the well-known novelist in four plays, none of which have achieved lasting fame.

In 1898 his two volumes of collected verse were published, followed in 1900 by a small volume entitled *For England's Sake: Verses and Songs in Time of War*. It was in this volume that he presented a poem that became well known to his contemporaries and to later generations until the taste for poetry changed during this century.

> What have I done for you,
> England, my England?
> What is there I would not do,
> England, my own?

Apart from the occasional anthologized poem he has now been largely forgotten except for the entries in dictionaries of quotations where some of the lines from 'Invictus' (1875) are still recorded:

> In the fell clutch of circumstance
> I have not winced nor cried aloud

William Henley

William Henley

Under the bludgeonings of chance
My head is bloody, but unbowed.

and

It matters not how strait the gate,
How charged with punishments the scroll,

I am the master of my fate:
I am the captain of my soul.

Henley also helped to bring to the notice of the British public the work of the painter Whistler and the sculptor Rodin. It was Rodin who fashioned the bust on Henley's memorial in the crypt of St Paul's Cathedral. He died at Woking on 11 June 1903. His body was cremated and the ashes were taken to Cockayne Hatley, Bedfordshire.

Cecil Ballantine

Margaritae Sorori (1886)

A late lark twitters from the quiet skies;
And from the west,
Where the sun, his day's work ended,
Lingers as in content,
There falls on the old, gray city
An influence luminous and serene,
A shining peace.

The smoke ascends
In a rosy-and-golden haze. The spires
Shine, and are changed. In the valley
Shadows rise. The lark sings on. The sun,
Closing his benediction,
Sinks, and the darkening air
Thrills with a sense of the triumphing night –
Night with her train of stars
And her great gift of sleep.

So be my passing!
My task accomplished and the long day done,
My wages taken, and in my heart
some late lark singing
Let me be gathered to the quiet west,
The sundown splendid and serene,
Death.

Chapter Fifteen

John Middleton

Little is known of John Middleton's early life except that he received his training in the office of the York architect James Pigott Pritchett, whose daughter he later married. He is also believed to have worked for a while with Pritchett's son, also an architect, in his Darlington practice before moving to Cheltenham with his family in about 1860. Some local residents thought Middleton had come to Cheltenham to retire, but soon realized they were mistaken when he opened an office in Clarence Street, on the corner of the passage to the parish church, from where he ran a successful practice for the next quarter of a century.

All Saints Church as it would have looked with its completed tower and spire

Middleton came to Cheltenham at a time of considerable building activity, and his five churches, for which he is best remembered today, were designed to serve the rapidly expanding residential areas on the fringes of this fashionable spa town. Spanning his whole career as a local architect, the five churches are all good examples of the Gothic Revival, a predilection undoubtedly inherited from Pritchett who favoured this style for his many Yorkshire churches and public buildings. The earliest of Middleton's churches, St Mark's, Lansdown (1860–6), is the least sumptuous of the five, but was the only one to receive a feature

A Gloucestershire Gallery

An artist's impression of St Mark's Church, showing the magnificent tower and spire

originally intended for them all, a lofty tower and spire. The four later churches are All Saints, Pittville (1865–8), Holy Apostles, Charlton Kings (1866–71), St Stephen's, Tivoli (1873–83), and St Philip and St James, Leckhampton

John Middleton

John Middleton

(1879–82). The latter is distinguished by a partially completed tower and copper-covered saddleback with fleche but otherwise they are all rather alike in design, characterized externally by the use of heavy rusticated stone, the well-proportioned interiors enhanced by contrasting coloured stones and marbles and much ornate carving, decoration and statuary.

Of the five, All Saints, 'specifically built for High Church, Tractarian worship in a town dominated by the Low Church Evangelicals', is the largest and undoubtedly the finest of Middleton's churches. It has been described as his most 'sumptuous masterpiece', and as 'a splendid example of what Sir Gilbert Scott was always aiming at and never achieved, complete Gothic self assurance and

Victorian punch'. Middleton originally planned a 200-ft tower and spire at the south-western corner, intending to make the church 'architecturally considered, the most ecclesiastical edifice in Cheltenham', but this was never completed.

Middleton's vision of creating for the town a medieval skyline of towers and spires was never to be fully realized, but his five churches, for which he appears to have charged no fees, stand today as his finest achievement and most significant contribution to Cheltenham's Victorian architecture.

Of the many architects practising in Gloucestershire during the second half of the nineteenth century, Middleton was one of the most talented and certainly one of the most prolific. He carried out alterations and extensions to many existing churches, including St Luke's and Holy Trinity in Cheltenham, and St Peter's, Leckhampton. He built new churches at Walton Cardiff, near Tewkesbury (now demolished), at Clearwell and at Oxenhall and was also responsible for major building projects at Cheltenham College, the Ladies' College, and the Delancey Hospital. He also supervised many works from his London office at Storey's Gate in Westminster.

Few details are known of Middleton's personal character or private life. A photograph portrays him as a rather grave and patriarchal figure, but he must have been a competent teacher, for a number of his assistants and pupils later achieved considerable distinction in the architectural profession, both in this country and overseas.

Following his sudden death in February 1885, Middleton's practice was briefly taken over by his only surviving son, John Henry.

Hugh Greenhalf

Chapter Sixteen

Isaac Pitman

The inventor of the best known system of shorthand, Isaac Pitman, was born in Trowbridge, Wiltshire, on 4 January 1813, the third of the 11 children of Samuel and Maria Pitman.

Isaac's younger brother, Benjamin, recalled that 'Isaac, in his youth, was of a diligent and studious habit. He was of a sensitive nature, inclined to be thoughtful, regarding life and its duties as matters of grave concern'. Isaac suffered fainting fits, because of his school's overcrowded conditions, so his father withdrew him when he was 13. He began work as a clerk in the cloth factory where his father was overseer. Isaac continued his studies at home, with his brother Jacob, rising at four in the morning and working again in the evenings. He was particularly interested in grammar and pronunciation, and began to study Taylor's shorthand system.

In 1829 Samuel Pitman started his own cloth manufacturing business. Isaac worked in the office until 1831, when his father sent him to the British and Foreign Schools Society Training College, Borough Road, London. After five months' training he took the post of master in a school in Barton-on-Humber, near Hull. He was then 19. Four years later he married Mrs Mary Holgate, widow of a Barton solicitor.

Meanwhile, in Wotton-under-Edge, a meeting on 24 November 1835 resolved 'to open schools for the better education of children and to start with the boys'. Isaac's brother, Jacob, who had also trained as a teacher, was by then master of a school in North Nibley, three miles from Wotton. He was a committee member, and proposed Isaac as master of the new school. So, in January 1836, aged 23, Isaac Pitman came to Gloucestershire.

On the journey from Barton he entered into conversation with a fellow traveller, which led to a discussion on the unorthodox theologian Swedenborg's ideas and Pitman became greatly influenced by his writings. Later in the year he admitted

Isaac Pitman

to the British School committee that he had changed his belief in the doctrine of the Trinity, having accepted that of Swedenborgianism, commonly known as the New Church. The committee thought this 'very unscriptural' and, 'as he would not promise to keep his sentiments from the boys', he was dismissed.

Isaac Pitman had been a very successful schoolmaster. After his dismissal from the British School, Pitman started his own private school, to which many of the boys from the British School transferred. He wanted to teach shorthand, but the cheapest books were beyond the boys' pockets, so he set about writing a cheap edition of Taylor's system. The publisher rejected it, advising him to produce his own system.

This he did, drawing on his earlier studies of the English language. He knew well the discrepancies between the written and the spoken word, and the shortcoming of the various systems of reporting speech.

On 15 November 1837, the first supply of Pitman's shorthand was ready under the title of 'Stenographic Sound-Hand'. Isaac's brother, Benjamin, who helped in the school, recorded in his diary, 'I have no doubt it will be practised almost universally in a short time. I like our new system much better than the old one. Besides, it is so much shorter, plainer and easier to be read.'

Examples of Pitman's 'writing by sound'

A Gloucestershire Gallery

The Pitman Centenary Commemoration Dinners

ISAAC PITMAN (Aged 32 Years).
Painted by J.B. Keene.

SIR ISAAC PITMAN.
Memorial Portrait by Sir Arthur S. Cope R.A.

EDINBURGH
The North British Station Hotel

BATH
Fortts.

LONDON
Grosvenor House

TROWBRIDGE
The Town Hall.

1937

WOTTON-under-EDGE
Swan Hotel.

Pitman continued to live and work in Wotton for another 18 months until, in June 1839, he moved to Bath, where he opened a 'school for young gentlemen'. The subjects included his own system of 'writing by sound'. He continued to develop and publish phonography, as it was now called, for over 50 years, his achievements being rewarded with a knighthood in 1894. After a period of ill health he died in Bath on 22 January 1897, aged 84.

Beryl Kingan

Chapter Seventeen

Dorothea Beale

A remarkable pioneer of opportunities for women lived and worked for 50 years in Gloucestershire. A visionary, believing passionately in the cause of emancipation, Dorothea Beale dedicated her life to achieving that end. Second Principal of the Cheltenham Ladies' College, founder of the Headmistresses Association, Vice-President of the Central Society for Womens' Suffrage, friend of John Ruskin, this Freeman of the Borough of Cheltenham was a trail-blazer. She dreamed of Esperanto and of the creation of a University of Cheltenham but not even this redoubtable lady could make all her dreams come true.

Born in 1831 into a Gloucestershire family, the child of a London doctor, she was tutored at home until, at 17, she went to school in Paris. Talented and deeply religious, she possessed a strong sense of vocation. When civil war ended her brief sojourn in France, she attended Queen's College, London, and there progressed speedily from pupil to headteacher by the age of 23.

Dorothea was attractive and charismatic, her sober exterior hiding a sense of fun and a child-like joyous nature. She was an excellent communicator and became a successful writer early in her career. Her gift of inspiring confidence gained for her collaboration, respect and affection as she initiated outstanding changes in the field of education.

Promotion was rapid and in her next headship at Casterton, a school for clergy daughters (immortalized as 'Lowood' in *Jane Eyre*) she had her first real clash of values. True to her beliefs she left, willingly, after a year.

In 1858 she was appointed principal of the Cheltenham Ladies' College, then a small school of about eighty pupils based in Cambray House. Her conviction that education for women should be as intellectually exacting and satisfying as for boys led to the inclusion of Greek, Science and Physical Education in her curriculum – not, however, without opposition. Many thought that girls had smaller brains than boys and would not cope with a similar curriculum. Some parents

A Gloucestershire Gallery

Dorothea Beale characteristically holding the flower emblem of the Ladies' College

Dorothea Beale

Photograph of girls in the science laboratory at the turn of the century

feared that by studying similar subjects to boys their girls would become too masculine and fail to make suitable marriages. Having turned down the opportunity more than once, Dorothea knew that not all women marry and that a sound education was a good basis for earning a living. Rumours spread that physical education would damage the reproductive organs. Miss Beale persevered. Modesty, deportment and decorum were taught. Historic heroines were cited as good examples to follow.

Before breakfast Miss Beale took a three-mile walk and, at the age of 67 with gout-stricken hands, she learned to ride a tricycle. The autocratic lady pedalled up Montpellier accompanied by a young, white-gloved page boy pushing hard on the saddle. He would receive free lessons for his efforts.

Numbers grew, scope widened, and in 1873 the Principal moved her 'husband', the College, to its present site at Royal Well. As time passed it became possible to enter the Kindergarten Department at three and to leave the Examination Class with a degree, all without leaving Cheltenham. St Hilda, Miss Beale's heroine, was commemorated in three of her foundations: a house for advanced students in Cheltenham, a hall of residence in Oxford and a Settlement in Bethnal Green, London, run by the Guild, an organization of old pupils. Through the Guild the influence of Dorothea Beale spread to all corners of the world.

A Gloucestershire Gallery

In 1906, mourned by her 'spiritual family', Dorothea Beale died. A memorial service in St Paul's Cathedral coincided with her funeral in Gloucester Cathedral where on 16 November, the eve of St Hilda's Day, she was laid to rest.

Ann Mentz

Chapter Eighteen

Benjamin Baker

Sir Benjamin Baker (1840–1907), Civil Engineer, was born at Keyford, Frome, Somerset on 31 March 1840, the son of Benjamin Baker and Sarah Hollis. His father, a native of County Carlow, Eire, became principal assistant at the ironworks in Tondu, Glamorgan, and no doubt this appointment had a great influence

The building of the Forth Bridge

Benjamin Baker

on young Benjamin in determining his future career. Baker was only four years old when he was brought to Cheltenham. He lived with his mother at Farm Cottage, 4 Cambray Place, before moving to No. 3 in 1854 and was educated at Cheltenham Grammar School. At the age of 16, he was apprenticed to H.H. Price of the Neath Abbey Ironworks for four years.

Moving to London in 1860, he served as assistant to W. Wilson on the construction of Grosvenor Road railway bridge and Victoria Station. In 1861 he joined the permanent staff of (Sir) John Fowler, became his partner in 1875, and was associated with him until Fowler's death in 1898. As a consulting engineer, he rapidly gained the highest reputation for skill and sagacity, and was consulted by the British and Egyptian governments, by the colonies, and by municipal and other corporations. The credit of the design and execution of the great constructional engineering achievements with which Baker's name is associated was necessarily shared by him with Fowler and many other colleagues, but Baker's judgment and resource were highly important factors in the success of these undertakings.

Baker became engaged on the underground railways of London. From 1861 he was employed on the construction of the Metropolitan (Inner Circle) railway and St Johns Wood extension, and in 1869 he worked on the construction of the District Railway from Westminster to the City. Baker was also consulting engineer for the first 'tube' railway, the City and South London line opened in 1890, and the Central London 'tube' railway opened in 1890, and in 1896 he was joint engineer for the Baker Street and Waterloo 'tube' railway.

From the early years of his career, Baker studied deeply the theory of construction and the resistance of materials. He wrote a series of articles on long span

Benjamin Baker's living model, with Mr Watanabe in the middle

bridges in 1867, and another 'On the Strength of Beams, Columns and Arches' in 1868 for *Engineering*. In his work on long span bridges he reached the conclusion that the maximum possible span would necessitate the adoption of cantilevers supporting an independent girder, the system later adopted for the Forth Bridge with which Baker was involved. The building of the Forth Bridge began in 1883 and was completed in 1890. Baker's services were rewarded by the honour of KCMG on 17 April 1890.

When the Forth Bridge was under construction, Baker devised a human demonstration to illustrate the way in which it worked. Two men sat on chairs with their arms outstretched and propped up by broom handles, thus forming models of cantilevers. Between them a seat was suspended, on which a third person could comfortably sit, his weight being counterbalanced by piles of bricks hung on the other side of his supporters. A classic picture was taken of this set-up with Kaichi Watanabe, a Japanese civil engineer, born in 1858, as the central figure. He had been sent by the Japanese Government to study at Glasgow University, and afterwards became one of the assistant engineers on the bridge. Baker chose him to appear in the photograph to mark the oriental origin of the cantilever principle.

This great railway bridge is its own testimonial to the perceptiveness and engineering genius of its designer, and in the view of the present-day Forth Bridge engineer, given adequate maintenance, it will still be there as robust as ever in another century from now. Baker was also responsible for many engineering projects in Egypt, the most renowned of which is the Aswan Dam which stretches 6,400 ft in length.

Baker died suddenly from syncope at his residence, Bowden Green in Pangbourne, Berkshire on 19 May 1907. He was buried at Idbury, near Chipping Norton.

Brian Nottingham

Chapter Nineteen

Edward Wilson

Dr Edward Adrian Wilson (1872–1912), scientist, artist, and Antarctic explorer, was born at 6 (now 91) Montpellier Terrace, Cheltenham on 23 July 1872, the son of a consulting physician at Cheltenham General Hospital.

Educated at Cheltenham's Glyngarth School, and as a day-boy at Cheltenham College, 'Ted', as he was known to his family, went to Cambridge in 1891, to read science and medicine, and graduated BA with first class honours in 1894. He then completed his medical training at London's St George's Hospital and

The statue of Edward Wilson in the Promenade, Cheltenham, sculpted, appropriately, by Captain Scott's widow, Kathleen, in 1914

Edward Wilson

received the degree of MB from Cambridge in 1900.

Wilson was a man of remarkably wide interests and ability, in whom a love of nature, inspired no doubt by the countryside around his boyhood home at the Crippetts, near Cheltenham, and a deep Christian faith were all-pervading. A highly accomplished artist, Wilson produced innumerable drawings and watercolours, mainly landscapes and naturalist subjects. His many Antarctic paintings stand alongside Herbert Ponting's famous photographs as a vivid record of his two journeys to the Antarctic. Among his less well-known achievements was his important research into grouse disease.

It is, however, for his contribution to Captain Scott's two British Antarctic expeditions that Wilson is most widely remembered. He joined the first expedition (the 1901–4 'Discovery' expedition) as second medical officer, vertebrate zoologist and artist, and soon established himself as one of Scott's closest companions, as well as a man who could inspire men of all ranks, so much so that he eventually became known to all simply as 'Bill'. Along with Scott and Shackleton, he journeyed to within 420 miles of the South Pole before Shackleton's illness forced them to turn back.

Given Wilson's positive contribution to the 1901–4 expedition, it is not surprising that Scott invited him to join the second expedition, in the 'Terra Nova', as chief of scientific staff. As during the previous expedition, much important scientific work was undertaken, culminating in a second attempt to reach the Pole, undertaken by a party of five men, including Wilson, in 1911–12. The South Pole was in fact reached on 17 January 1912, although the sense of achievement must have been lessened by the sight of the Norwegian flag already flying at the spot, Amundsen having reached the Pole several weeks before.

The following day, the Pole party set off to return to their camp at Cape Evans, and both Scott's and Wilson's diaries record their gradual deterioration in the face of terrible weather, food and fuel shortages, and sickness. Scott, Wilson, and Bowers were the last to survive, and died together in their tent in late March 1912, 155 miles from Cape Evans. There they were found, and buried, eight months later. Two years later, Cheltenham commemorated one of its most illustrious sons with a statue in the Promenade, sculpted, appropriately, by Captain Scott's widow, Kathleen.

Steven Blake

Overleaf: Antarctic watercolour by Edward Wilson

Chapter Twenty
James Elroy Flecker

The name James Elroy Flecker is well-known to local poets and staff of Dean Close School but few other people in Cheltenham are aware that Flecker was a national poet resident in Cheltenham. This lack of acknowledgment of a local poet by Cheltonians is surprising although Flecker was away a great deal on his travels.

Herman James Elroy Flecker was born in Lewisham, London on 5 November 1884. He came to Cheltenham at the age of two when his father Dr William Flecker was appointed the first headmaster of Dean Close School. He was sent away to Uppingham School in 1901 where he was considered to be a brilliant student, and within two years had won an open scholarship in Classics to Trinity College, Oxford. At Oxford, however, the bright young man, known for his wit and conversation, let his studies suffer and obtained a third class degree. He left Oxford in 1906 to take up the first of a number of positions as a schoolmaster. A year later he published his first volume of poetry, *The Bridge of Fire*. Flecker craved for adventure and soon tired of teach-

James Elroy Flecker

James Elroy's father Dr William Flecker, the first headmaster of Dean Close School

ing, deciding instead on a career in the consular service in the hope of travel and a posting abroad. In preparation for this change of career, Flecker entered Caius College, Cambridge where he studied Oriental languages with the aim of gaining an interpreter's qualification.

At Cambridge Flecker mixed with people of a flamboyant nature whose conduct and morality were unconventional. His contemporaries included the historian Oscar Browning; the writer of homosexual literature, Frederick William Rolfe, or 'Baron Corvo' as he was known; and the writer of risqué novels, Ronald Firbank. Flecker was considered to be an aesthete with a passion to shock, particularly with obscenity. In his attempts to be original, Flecker joined the Fabians where he met the young Rupert Brooke. They both attended a summer school held by the leading Fabians of the time, Sidney and Beatrice Webb. Brooke and Flecker were not great friends. Flecker was by no means an ardent Socialist, and his interest in the Fabians lay in a young woman named Eleanor Finlayson. Although a proposal of marriage he made to Eleanor was accepted, their engagement only lasted a few weeks.

In June 1910 Flecker left England to start his love–hate relationship with the Middle East, taking up the post of vice-consul in Constantinople. It was also at this time that the tuberculosis that was to plague him for the rest of his life was diagnosed. He had only been in the Middle East four months when he had to return home. He stayed in a sanatorium in Cranham where he wrote the poem 'Oak and Olive'. While in England he also published *Thirty-six Poems* and *The Grecians*.

During a stay in Europe, Flecker visited Paris where he finished his play *Don Juan*. He returned to Constantinople in March 1911, believing himself to be

James Elroy Flecker

A family group taken in 1906 on the occasion of the Silver Wedding of Dr and Mrs Flecker. James can be seen in the centre back

cured. In April he was transferred to Smyrna where he was taken ill again. Not long after his relationship with Eleanor Finlayson, which was followed by a brief affair with another woman, he married a Greek woman, Helle Siardaressia, whom he had met on the boat to Constantinople.

Flecker did not return to Smyrna, but was instead transferred to Beirut as vice-consul. He had by now begun writing *Hassan* and had already published *Forty-two Poems*. Flecker was, however, drawing to an end his romantic love affair with the East, and tiring of the consular service. Unsuccessful in Beirut, he sought a teaching post back in Britain.

In 1912 the Fleckers moved to Areiya where they briefly met T.E. Lawrence, although a friendship did not develop between them. Lawrence took Flecker to be like many of the British in the East: they like it, but did not have that commitment or passion for the land or its people.

In 1913 there was a relapse in Flecker's health and he was sent to a sanatorium in Switzerland. It was there that he published the well-known volume of poems, *The Golden Journey to Samarkand* as well as writing and publishing his only novel, *The King of Alsander*. Flecker died on 3 January 1915 and his collected poems and prose were published posthumously.

Don Hale

A Gloucestershire Gallery

The Golden Journey to Samarkand

We who with songs beguile your pilgrimage
And swear that Beauty lives though lilies die,
    We Poets of the proud old lineage
Who sing to find your hearts, we know not why, –

What shall we tell you? Tales, marvellous tales
Of ships and stars and isles where good men rest,
    Where nevermore the rose of sunset pales,
And winds and shadows fall toward the West:

And there the world's first huge white-bearded kings
    In dim glades sleeping, murmur in their sleep,
And closer round their breasts the ivy clings,
    Cutting its pathway slow and red and deep.

And how beguile you? Death has no repose
    Warmer and deeper than that Orient sand
Which hides the beauty and bright faith of those
    Who made the Golden Journey to Samarkand.

And now they wait and whiten peaceably,
Those conquerors, those poets, those so fair:
They know time comes, not only you and I,
But the whole world shall whiten, here or there;

When those long caravans that cross the plain
    with dauntless feet and sound of silver bells
    Put forth no more for glory or for gain,
Take no more solace from the palm-girt wells.

When the great markets by the sea shut fast
All that calm Sunday that goes on and on:
When even lovers find their peace at last,
And Earth is but a star, that once had shone.

Chapter Twenty-One

John Nevil Maskelyne

John Nevil Maskelyne (1839–1917) is regarded as the father of modern magic. For many years his name was a household word in the field of entertainment. He was a single-minded man and a man of integrity who never ceased to expose card sharpers and fraudulent mediums. Maskelyne was also a brilliant inventor, and in this respect he assisted the Admiralty during the First World War by devising means whereby sailors in action could be protected from burns caused by gunfire. Such exceptional gifts are not altogether surprising. His ancestor Nevil Maskelyne was Astronomer Royal to George III and was the inventor of the prismatic compass. Nevil's sister Margaret was the wife of Clive of India.

The house in Cheltenham where Maskelyne was born was demolished long ago when the railway was extended across the lower end of the High Street, but a section of the little terrace still remains.

John Nevil Maskelyne

Being interested in mechanics, Maskelyne was apprenticed to a watch-maker in Montpellier. A tablet commemorating the site was unveiled

A Gloucestershire Gallery

Maskelyne's masterpiece Zoe, a young lady who could sketch any celebrity chosen by the audience

by the magician Paul Daniels in 1989.

John Nevil came to prominence through his exposure of the famous Davenport Brothers as fraudulent spiritualist mediums. The Brothers performed at the old Town Hall in Regent Street, and Maskelyne was a member of a committee

John Nevil Maskelyne

Maskelyne conducting one of his escape illusions

formed to monitor the performance. Later he repeated their performance by his own dexterity. This success led to his partnership with a friend, a young man name Cooke. Maskelyne and Cooke, as they came to be known, revolutionized professional magic as an entertainment, gaining a lasting reputation. Their show contained many baffling illusions and ingenious devices which caught the public's imagination. Later they set up at the Egyptian Hall, Piccadilly, which came to be known as England's Home of Mystery, dwarfing all rivals.

Maskelyne's mechanical genius produced some remarkable inventions, notably his automata, the most famous being Psycho which performed amazing feats and now resides in the British Museum. His masterpiece Zoe, a young lady who

A Gloucestershire Gallery

12 Rotunda Terrace, Montpellier, Cheltenham, where Maskelyne was apprenticed to a watch-maker

could sketch any celebrity chosen by the audience, however, never exceeded the popularity of Psycho. One of his most admired tricks was plate spinning, which he performed to perfection. The partners gave their first Royal Command performance at Sandringham before Prince Edward and Princess Alexandra.

Eventually Maskelyne moved from the Egyptian Hall and set up his own theatre at the St George's Hall, London, the site now occupied by the BBC. The programmes included other magicians and featured a number of effective playlets, the most famous being *Will, the Witch and the Watchman* which ran for 40 years. Maskelyne was the originator of the matinee. Maskelyne's second partner David Devant was one of the great British magicians.

Maskelyne's many inventions included a typewriter, of which the keyboard was adopted universally, devices for automatic switches for gas and electric lighting, penny-in-the-slot machines and a bus-ticket punch. He was also a pioneer in cinematic photography, producing one of the first newsreels of Queen Victoria's Diamond Jubilee.

Maskelyne was the first president of the Magic Circle, London, founded in 1905. His son Nevil took over the theatre when his father retired. His grandson Jasper followed the family tradition as a stage illusionist, and in the 1930s appeared at the Opera House in Cheltenham, now the Everyman Theatre.

Michael Seacome

Chapter Twenty-Two

Ashton Lister

Few people outside Gloucestershire are aware that the small town of Dursley boasts a diesel-engine factory whose products, which have also comprised air compressors, generating sets and construction and agricultural machinery, have been exported all over the world. R.A. Lister and Co., as the firm was originally called, is now part of the Lister–Petter division of Hawker Siddeley. How did such a major industry develop in an old woollen town?

The story begins with George Lister, who came from Yorkshire to Dursley in the 1820s. At that time the whole Stroud and Dursley region was still a major wool cloth producing area, and George started by making 'cards', wire brushes used in one of the preparatory processes. He went on to build up a large business producing machinery for the woollen industry, despite the fact that by the 1830s the Gloucestershire woollen industry itself was in permanent decline.

Sir Ashton Lister, knighted by George V in 1911

A Gloucestershire Gallery

George Lister

George's son, Robert Ashton, inherited his father's drive and business acumen. Born in 1845, he had an unusual education which incorporated spells abroad as well as technical training. He briefly entered his father's firm, but each man's strong character quickly led to an irreparable personal rift. Ashton Lister then set up his own firm, R.A. Lister and Co., in 1867.

Ashton started making agricultural machinery, a growing industry at that time due to agricultural mechanization. In the 1890s, the firm grew substantially as it started manufacturing a Danish-designed cream-separator,

Some early Lister dairy equipment, 1896. The cream separator, which did so much to aid the growth of the company, can be seen in the centre foreground

Ashton Lister

Employees of R.A. Lister and Co. Ltd returning to work after dinner in 1914, photographed in Long Street, Dursley. Long Street leads from Dursley town centre down into the valley where Lister's factory was located

which speeded up the age-old process of skimming the cream from the whey, as a first stage in butter-making. The separator proved an inestimable boon for farmers throughout the world, and Lister's output grew rapidly. By the 1900s they produced their own design of separator, and added sheep-shearing machinery to their product range.

Until the late nineteenth century, agricultural machinery had been powered by hand, by horse or sometimes by steam. By now Ashton's sons Austin and Charles were playing an important part in the firm, and after the First World War Charles' sons were to join them. In an episode curiously reminiscent of the estrangement between Ashton and his father, a dispute between Charles and his sons ended in Charles leaving the firm in 1925. The guiding spirit of the firm became his third son Charles Percy Lister, always known as Percy.

Under Percy Lister the firm became one of the first to manufacture small, light diesels. Lister and Co.'s diesels became an instant success as a more economical substitute for petrol engines with many applications. Throughout the Depression of the 1930s Listers, and Dursley, boomed. Indeed Dursley boasted one of the

A Gloucestershire Gallery

A Lister petrol engine, 1909

lowest rates of unemployment in those difficult years. Diesels were the mainstay, although other products were developed such as the well-known Lister range of garden furniture. This stemmed from the firm's involvement in making wooden butter churns. Lister's success continued until they were taken over by Hawker Siddeley in 1965.

Fittingly, Ashton Lister survived until 1929, when the diesel engine range was launched. As well as pursuing his business career, he and his wife Frances were active benefactors of many local causes, and strong supporters of the Congregational Church. These and his political activities led to a knighthood in 1911. As a keen Liberal, he fulfilled a long-held ambition by his election as MP for Stroud in 1918. Nevertheless his main claim to fame remains the business he founded.

Charles More

The author would like to acknowledge the use of the following sources: David Evans, *Listers, The First Hundred Years*, Alan Sutton, 1979; Charles More, 'Sir Charles Percy' in D.J. Jeremy (ed.), *The Dictionary of Business Biography*, 1985.

Chapter Twenty-Three
Gustav Holst

Gustav Holst (1874–1934), best known as the composer of 'The Planets', was born and educated in Cheltenham. He is remembered in his home town by the Holst Birthplace Museum, a period house containing some of his scores and memorabilia of his life.

Born in a small house in the former Pittville Terrace, the son of a local musician, Holst's childhood was not the happiest. His mother died when he was seven and he was brought up by his father's sister who was undomesticated but taught him to play the piano. He suffered from chronic asthma and very poor eyesight although no-one realized at the time that he needed glasses. His father later remarried.

Gustav was sent to the Cheltenham Grammar School, then situated in the Lower High Street. His stepmother was a Theosophist and her views made an impression on the young mind. This led to Holst's interest in Hinduism and Astrology, influences evident in some of his major works.

Holst's birthplace in Clarence Road, now the Holst Birthplace Museum

A Gloucestershire Gallery

Gustav Holst

He started his working life as the organist at Wyck Rissington before the success of a local operetta 'Lansdown Castle' encouraged his father to send him to the Royal College of Music, where he was awarded a scholarship for composition in 1895. While attending the College he earned the respect of Parry and commenced a life-long friendship with Vaughan Williams. Due to neuritis in his right arm he learnt to play the trombone and in 1898 he joined the Carl Rosa Opera Company as repetiteur and then spent several seasons playing in the Scottish Orchestra. It was during this time that he married Isobel Harrison, a girl he met

Bedroom in the Holst Birthplace Museum

when he conducted the Hammersmith Socialist Choir as a student. He also had his first real success as a composer with his 'Cotswold Symphony' in 1902 at the Bournemouth Winter Gardens.

In 1903, Holst decided that he would give up the trombone and concentrate on composition. After some difficulties he began a successful career as a teacher at the James Allen's Girls' School at Dulwich, where he stayed until 1920. Two years later he also became Musical Director of St Paul's Girls' School in Hammersmith, which became a second home. There he was given a sound-proof room in which he did much of his composition. He remained in this post until his death in 1934.

Late in September 1918 Holst was given a private performance of his newly written 'The Planets' by a friend, Balfour Gardiner, before he took up a short assignment of war service with the YMCA in the Near East. On his return he became a professor at both the Royal College of Music and University College, Reading, although these posts were given up after illness in 1924.

The next few years saw a number of first public performances of major works including 'The Planets' (1919), 'The Hymn of Jesus' (1920), and his opera 'The Perfect Fool' (1923).

Holst returned in triumph to his home town in 1927 when he was honoured with a concert of his works at the Town Hall by the Birmingham Orchestra. Despite ill health he was able to conduct a complete performance of 'The Planets'.

A Gloucestershire Gallery

The 1887 Cheltenham Grammar School, then situated in the Lower High Street, as it would have appeared during Holst's schooldays

This, and the 1931 performance of his 'Choral Fantasia' at the Three Choirs Festival, were to be Holst's last important visits to Gloucestershire. He died in 1934 and his ashes were interred in Chichester Cathedral.

Andrew Mulford

Chapter Twenty-Four

The Martyns

H.H. Martyn (1841–1937) founded the internationally renowned decorative artwork company H.H. Martyn and Co. in 1888. The company was the biggest employer in Cheltenham for decades, expanding to over a thousand men by 1920, by which time the Gloster Aircraft Co. had evolved from Martyns and was employing another one thousand personnel, both companies having a great influence on the prosperity of Cheltenham and Gloucester.

Herbert Martyn was a man with a social conscience. He assisted in the formation and running of Cheltenham's Working Men's College (1883–1900) which was closely affiliated to Cheltenham Ladies' College and the Boys' College. With the Revd J. Owen he also helped found a mission (1870) in Rutland Street, Cheltenham, where the very poor were provided with food, warmth and social entertainment.

H.H. Martyn was born in Lych Street, Worcester, the thirteenth and last child of his poverty-stricken parents who eked out their existence selling old clothes. His schooling was minimal and only made possible by the generosity of a lady who paid the 2d. per week charge, and who later also paid for a course at Worcester Art School, having recognized a talent in young Martyn.

He held a number of positions as a youngster including that of button polisher, errand boy, photographer's assistant and railway clerk. Eventually he came into the employ of James Forsyth, a stone and wood carver, who reintroduced him to the craft he had learnt at art school. Martyn later joined R.L. Boulton, with whom he worked on restoration stone carving for Worcester Cathedral. In 1866 he moved with his employer to Cheltenham to work on the many churches then under construction. In 1874 he formed a partnership with E.A. Emms, a stone mason.

In 1888 H.H. Martyn and Co. was founded with premises at the corner of College Road and the High Street, Cheltenham. The company's work was

A Gloucestershire Gallery

H.H. Martyn's own stone carving skills are present in this reredos executed soon after 1888, when he founded his company. Now in St Philips and St James Cheltenham, the design was by Middleton, Prothero and Philpott

*The founder of H.H. Martyn and Co., H.H. Martyn, aged 71
and his wife Fanny (née Clissold)*

A Gloucestershire Gallery

The interior of the SS Otranto. *The plasterwork, metalwork, furniture and decorative columns in the first class lounge were by H.H. Martyn and Co.*

comprehensive and included wood, stone and marble carving, modelling of decorative plaster enrichments, and casting in bronze and other metals. Within 10 years the company employed 200 craftsmen, 50 of whom were wood carvers. In 1917 Martyn was awarded the Royal Warrant for work at Buckingham Palace and Windsor Castle.

The fitting out of ships, including the *Titanic* and the Queen's liners, became a major part of the company's business. The company's work was also evident on trains such as the *Canadian Pacific*, *Orient Express*, King Farouk's train and the royal train for the Prince of Wales's tour of India in 1925.

H.H. Martyn was married for 53 years to Fanny Clissold. They had five sons and three daughters of whom only three sons and two daughters survived childhood. Their eldest son, Alfred W. Martyn was to have a profound influence on the company.

Alfred W. Martyn started work for his father as a stone mason at the age of 14, at 16 he attended evening classes at the Working Men's College, and by the age

The Martyns

of 30 he was managing director of H.H. Martyn and Co. It was his drive which led to the vast expansion of the company and its unique standing among its international clients.

In 1908 the company moved to Lansdown in Cheltenham where five acres of buildings enabled further expansion and larger scale bronze casting. At its height Martyns cast 75 per cent of all the art casting in this country.

Early in 1914 Martyns was chosen by the Aircraft Manufacturing Co. of Hendon to make wings and fuselages for Maurice Farman and De Haviland aircraft, and later for Bristol Fighters.

On 5 June 1917 A.W. Martyn formed a new company, the Gloucestershire Aircraft Co. (later named Gloster Aircraft Co.). Gloster Aircraft became famous for high speed flight, producing the first British aircraft to break the 200 mph barrier in 1922. The company had many successes, building aircraft to compete in the Schneider Trophy contests, and designing and building the first Allied jet aircraft to fly and the Allies' only jet aircraft to go into active service.

A.W. Martyn was involved in the life of Cheltenham in a number of other ways including as chairman of the Governors of the North Gloucestershire Technical College for 13 years, county councillor, member of Charlton Kings Urban District Council, chairman of the Children's Hospital Committee and Commissioner for the Inland Revenue.

View of Sunningend factory, Cheltenham

A Gloucestershire Gallery

Erecting shop in the Sunningend factory, Cheltenham, of H.H. Martyn. Mars VI Nighthawks (1922) are being finished for Nos 1 and 8 Squadrons

A.W. Martyn, founder of the Gloster Aircraft Co.

A.W. Martyn made a tremendous impact on local industry through his involvement in the early years of Dowty Equipment Ltd. He became chairman of Dowtys in 1936, a position he held until his death in 1947. It was A.W. Martyn's prompt financial intervention in the early years that kept Dowtys in Cheltenham and ensured that the tough Dowty aircraft undercarriages were ready in quantity at the outbreak of war. A.W. Martyn's time at Dowty's witnessed a dramatic increase in orders and the number employed in factories not only in Cheltenham but also in Canada and the United States.

A.W. Martyn married Ada, daughter of Steven Newman, a basket maker of Maisemore, Gloucester. They had two daughters and a son.

John Whitaker

Chapter Twenty-Five

Ivor Gurney

'Willy, Willy, I have done 5 of the most delightful and beautiful songs you ever cast your beaming eyes upon. They are all Elizabethan the words and blister my Kidneys, bisurate my magnesia if the music is not as English, as joyful, as tender as any lyric of all that noble host'. So wrote Ivor Gurney to his best friend, the poet F.W. Harvey, in July 1914. He had been a student at the Royal College of Music for three years and was producing work of outstanding quality. His tutor Sir Charles Villiers Stanford was to say of him that of all his pupils, which included Vaughan Williams, Ireland, Bliss and many more, Gurney was potentially 'the biggest of them all. But the least teachable'. Today, Ivor Gurney is recognized not only as one of the finest composers of song that this country has produced, but also as one of the major figures in English poetry of this century.

Ivor Gurney

Ivor Gurney was born at 3 Queen Street (now Queen's Way), Gloucester, the son of a tailor, on 28 August 1890. Shortly after his birth, Gurney's family moved to shop premises at 19 Barton Street.

A Gloucestershire Gallery

All Saints' Church, Barton Street, Gloucester, where Gurney sang in the choir as a boy

As a boy, Gurney sang in the choir of All Saints' Church, Barton Street, and in 1900 became a Gloucester Cathedral chorister, later becoming an articled pupil of Dr (later Sir) Herbert Brewer, the Gloucester Cathedral organist. During these years he met his life-long friends F.W. Harvey and the composer Herbert Howells, who was also studying with Brewer. With them he shared in the joy of Gloucestershire, of walking the Cotswolds and the Severn Vale. With Harvey he also shared in the discovery of the Elizabethans: Fletcher, Nashe, Marlowe, and especially of Ben Jonson and Shakespeare.

Gurney's inspiration was built upon the foundation stone of his love for his country, his sense of being part of a continuum with its roots in Roman Gloucester, and self-identification with his English masters, Jonson in poetry and Byrd in music.

From childhood Gurney struggled with an awareness of mental instability; of disturbing mood swings which interrupted his otherwise joyous spirit. Even so, when war came in 1914, he tried to enlist in the Glosters alongside F.W. Harvey. He was rejected due to defective eyesight, but was accepted in February 1915 when, of necessity, Army entry standards had fallen.

Before leaving for France, a bookstall find in Gloucester purchased by a near-

Ivor Gurney

Ivor Gurney's grave, Twigworth Parish Church, near Gloucester

penniless Gurney for fourpence ('For fourpence to me was bankruptcy then or worse') was Walt Whitman's *Leaves of Grass*. Gurney was 'taken like a flood', Whitman 'whose page is coloured with earth's and his heart's blood', fired his imagination and became a dominant influence in a struggle to bestride the languages of the Old World and the New. The struggle was to result in the achievement of a poetic voice of absolute originality.

A Gloucestershire Gallery

In the trenches Gurney's creative energy was channelled into the writing of verse, there being very little opportunity for musical composition. Even so, a few songs were written, including two which perfectly expressed his longing for Gloucestershire: a setting of *In Flanders* by F.W. Harvey, and *Severn Meadows*, Gurney's only published song-setting of his own verse.

> Only the wanderer
> Knows England's graces,
> Or can anew see clear
> Familiar faces.
>
> And who loves joy as he
> That dwells in shadows?
> Do not forget me quite,
> O Severn meadows.

Two other trench songs are also valedictory in nature. One is a setting of John Masefield's poem, 'By a Bierside', and the other of Sir Walter Raleigh's farewell to life, 'Even Such is Time'. All four songs are undoubted masterpieces.

In September 1917, Gurney was gassed at Passchendaele and invalided home. His mental condition caused his friends and family grave concern. There were threats of suicide. However, by March 1919 he was fit enough to return to the Royal College of Music, this time to study with Vaughan Williams.

Now followed one of the happiest, most fruitful and creative period of Gurney's life. In the second half of 1919 he set over forty songs and wrote a number of instrumental pieces. The outpouring continued through 1920, but then the moods of depression increased once more. His behaviour became increasingly erratic. In the summer of 1921 he finally left the RCM and returned to Gloucestershire. By 1922 his eccentricity had become intolerable to his family. Before the end of the year he had been committed to the City of London Mental Hospital at Dartford, Kent, to remain there for 15 years until his death on 26 December 1937 at the age of 47.

Ivor Gurney is buried in the churchyard of Twigworth Parish Church, close to Gloucester.

Anthony Boden

Chapter Twenty-Six

Gilbert Jessop

Gilbert Laird Jessop, man of Gloucestershire and brilliant world famous cricketer, was known as 'the Croucher' because of his stance at the wicket but undoubtedly 'Panther' would have been a more apt title. Crouch he certainly did for style meant nothing to him, but his certain eye and speed of foot were so amazing that he could do all the unorthodox things of life and continue to succeed. There has never been another player of his type who was so successful. As a fielder he was magnificent, he ranked highly as a fast bowler and he was the most ruthlessly unorthodox destroyer of bowling hopes that cricket has ever known.

The birth of Gilbert Jessop on 19 May 1874 completed, as he says in his autobiography, 'a full Jessop eleven'. There was however no particular cricket tradition in the family, although his father Dr H.E. Jessop, a medical practitioner of No. 30 Cambray Place, Cheltenham, had various sporting assets, not the least being a natural flick of the wrist and great speed and agility despite being a man of 18 stone.

The young Gilbert first practised his cricket in the small confines of an eight square yard garden, and as the surgery windows bounded the 'off' side of the small pitch he soon developed a capacity for breaking windows which was to last him throughout his career. The only safe ground to play on was a passageway which can still be seen.

When he was 11, Jessop entered Cheltenham Grammar School where he was noticed by the headmaster as a born games player and soon won his First Eleven colours, becoming the chief bowler while still only 13. On the death of his father in 1890 he had to unfortunately leave school early but continued playing in village matches.

A post as assistant master at Alvechurch Grammar School in Worcestershire was followed by another at a school in South Woodford in Essex which proved to be a milestone in his career: he scored his first century which he described as

A Gloucestershire Gallery

Gilbert Laird Jessop, by A. Chevallier Tayler, 1905

No. 30 Cambray Place, birthplace of Jessop

A Gloucestershire Gallery

'a great event in a cricketer's life'.

After that he returned to the region to teach, this time in Burford. One story from these days tells of a local club which reluctantly told him that he could no longer play for them because he lost so many balls while batting. At his next job at Beccles College his remarkable performances made a great impact on W.G. Grace. In his first match for Cambridge University in 1896 his 'bouncers' came in for special censure in *The Times*.

By 1900 Jessop's cricket was placed on a different footing with his appointment as county captain. Previously he had made his debut for Gloucestershire in 1894 against Lancashire at Old Trafford, but now he was no longer the university amateur helping his county after the end of term. During his 12 years as captain he scored 53 first-class uninhibited centuries made at lightning speed, providing spectators with wonderful thrills which drew eager crowds to Gloucestershire's games.

Of his 18 Test appearances he scored only one century, in 1902, in what is known as 'Jessop's Match'. In 75 minutes on a rain-damaged wicket he scored 104 thus winning the game for England.

He played his last game for Gloucestershire in 1914 and after being invalided out of the army in 1917, spent his final 20 years at his son's house in Dorset where he died in 1955.

Keith Ball

Chapter Twenty-Seven

George Dowty

Sir George Herbert Dowty (1901–75), aeronautical engineer, inventor, and industrialist, was born on 27 April 1901 at Pershore, Worcestershire, the son of William Dowty, a chemist in Pershore, and his wife Laura Masters, who was from a family long established in the Vale of Evesham. He was the elder of twin brothers by half an hour, and the seventh son in the family. In so large a family there was no money to spare with which to spoil the little boy by giving expensive toys, but after his father's death, he was befriended by his brother-in-law, Sidney Fizroy Fell, a Worcester solicitor. It was Fell who first awakened Dowty's interest in things mechanical by giving him his most treasured possession, a small toy steam engine. Dowty recalled how he contrived a miniature set of fairground 'gallopers' for the steam engine to drive, making ingenious use of an old umbrella in the process.

Dowty's education commenced at a small private school in Pershore until 1913, when he entered Worcester Royal Grammar School, which he was obliged to leave at the age of 14 because his older brothers had been conscripted into the Army, and he had to help in running the various family businesses. At the age of 12 Dowty lost his right eye during some experiments with photographic materials when a bottle of magnesium powder exploded.

He began his engineering career in Worcester by joining the old and famous firm of Heenan & Froude at a wage of six shillings per week. His first job, pressure testing, using a hydraulic hand pump, the cast-iron cylinder for aero-engines, introduced him to hydraulics, which were later to be so important to him. Realizing his need for a special engineering education he began what became a lifetime study and joined evening classes at the local Victoria Institute, paying his own fees. In July 1918 Dowty obtained a new job as a draughtsman with British Aerial Transport in London. The company's chief designer was Bobby Noordvyn, a Dutchman and a pioneer of aircraft design in Britain and later in

A Gloucestershire Gallery

Canada. Dowty, eager to learn, worked on undercarriages, and in Noordvyn's creative environment, accelerated his career rapidly and perhaps impatiently. He then moved and gained considerable experience with a number of companies, including A.V. Roe at Hamble where he specialized in undercarriages in the design office.

Dowty came to Gloucestershire in 1924 on joining Gloster Aircraft Co., where he rapidly established his reputation as an aeronautical engineer. At the end of June 1931, he resigned from that company, and set up the Aircraft Components Co., borrowed against a life assurance, and established single-handed the first foundations of a vast international engineering enterprise. He received his first order from Kawasaki of Japan for internally sprung undercarriage wheels, so with this one order, no factory, but sub-contract manufacture and the help in the evening of two friends, Dowty designed, ordered, and assembled two of his wheels, and within nine weeks shipped them to Japan, being paid on shipment. His first business premises was a mews loft at 10 Lansdown Terrace Lane, Cheltenham, then Grosvenor Place South, and eventually in 1935 Arle Court, Cheltenham, which became both the company headquarters and Dowty's home.

During the Second World War Dowty's inventive and creative engineer's mind

10 Lansdown Terrace Lane, Cheltenham, where Dowty began his first business

George Dowty beside an undercarriage test bed

A Gloucestershire Gallery

Arle Court, Cheltenham, Dowty's home and company headquarters from 1935

was fully unleashed. Twenty-eight different aircraft were fitted with Dowty equipment, which included 12,900 sets for Hurricane, over 90,000 other undercarriages units, and over one million hydraulic units. Plants were set up throughout Britain and in Canada and the USA.

After the war Dowty applied his new approaches to hydraulics to wider fields – motor cycle forks, hydraulic pit props, industrial pumps, and hydraulic control systems, in the process of which many other companies were acquired.

Dowty was knighted in 1956. He was also the president of the Royal Aeronautical Society and the Society of British Aircraft Constructors. He received honorary doctorates from Bath University and Cranfield Institute of Technology, and was made freeman of Cheltenham (1955) and Tewkesbury (1964).

In 1948 Dowty had married Marguerite Anne Gowans of Newmarket, Ontario, Canada. They had a son and daughter. Dowty died on 7 December 1975 at his home on the Isle of Man.

Brian Nottingham

Chapter Twenty-Eight
C. Day Lewis

Cecil Day Lewis is best known in the world of literature as one quarter of 'MacSpauday', that mythical creature who dominated English poetry of the 1930s and who is deemed to epitomize much of the naivety, idealism and political turbulence of that troubled decade. This creature, it should be added, also produced much of the finest writing of the period. Day Lewis' contribution was not inconsiderable and was produced during his eight year residency in Cheltenham which began in 1930 when he arrived in the Regency town as a junior teacher. When he left he was one of the best-known poets in the land as well as a successful writer of detective fiction.

C. Day Lewis

The poet was born at Ballintubbert, Ireland in 1904. His father was a Church of Ireland curate and although the family moved to England when Cecil was only 18 months old, he remained proud of his Irish connection throughout his life. He was educated at Sherborne and at Wadham College, Oxford, and by the time he was appointed as a teacher of Classics in English at Cheltenham Junior College he had published two volumes of verse with the third, the important *Transitional Poem*, awaiting publication.

With his wife of 16 months, Mary, he moved into a miserable flat in Belmore

A Gloucestershire Gallery

Box Cottage in Bafford Lane, Charlton Kings, Cheltenham, where C. Day Lewis lived for 7 years

House, Bath Place, and began his stint as teacher in what was essentially the prep school for the senior college. He was, as accounts from ex-pupils testify, a popular and competent tutor but relations with colleagues and superiors were always strained. Being a poet was considered bad enough but when his political learning became known he was considered dangerously subversive.

His only ally was another misfit, the Kent and Gloucestershire batsman Lionel Hedges, who was games master at the college. Hedges was famous for his fondness for ale and the two cemented an alliance of outsiders night after night in the Beehive public house close to the college. Hedges' untimely death is the subject of the title poem 'A Time to Dance' (1935), one of Day Lewis' finest.

In 1931 the family (a son, Sean, was born April 1930) brought the freehold to Box Cottage, Charlton Kings, a small but charming house with superb views of the surrounding hills. This inaugurated a period of great productivity as Lewis' writing grew in confidence. His stay produced four volumes of verse: *From*

C. Day Lewis

Feather to Iron (1931), *The Magnetic Mountain* (1933), *A Time to Dance* (1936) and *Overtures to Death* (1938). Each one increased Day Lewis' reputation as one of the finest of the young 'committed' poets. He also produced the important critical work *A Hope for Poetry* (1934), a manifesto for the aims of the Auden/Spender/Day Lewis' group.

He left teaching in 1935 and to supplement his income turned to writing detective stories under the pseudonym of Nicholas Blade. These appeared annually and the first three were essentially pot-boilers. The fourth *The Beast Must Die* (1938) had a more original voice and is today considered a classic of the genre.

Day Lewis was actively involved in left-wing politics throughout this time. He was a leading member of the local Communist Party (1936–8) acting as education officer. His other main contribution to local life was as chairman of the newly-formed Cheltenham Literary Society.

His stay in Cheltenham ended when the Lewis' found their ideal home while on holiday in Devon. Lewis' subsequent career is well documented. In the war he worked for the Ministry of Information and in 1951 he was appointed Professor of Poetry at Oxford, the first poet of note to hold the post since Matthew Arnold. His reputation grew, apart from periodic fashionable hiccups, and in 1968 the ex-communist became Poet Laureate. He died in 1972.

Day Lewis' poetry, with its combination of lyricism and introspection and its variety of subject matter, retains its strength and accessibility today. Yet it is the body of work produced on the edge of the Cotswolds in the 1930s that established him as a major voice and which remains both his most typical and his most forceful.

Maurice Bottomley

A Gloucestershire Gallery

The Conflict

I sang as one
Who on a tilting deck sings
To keep their courage up, though the wave hangs
That shall cut off their sun.

As storm-cocks sing,
Flinging their natural answer in the wind's teeth,
And care not if it is waste of breath
Or birth-carol of spring.

As ocean-flyer clings
To height, to the last drop of spirit driving on
while yet ahead is land to be won
And work for wings.

Singing I was at peace,
Above the clouds, outside the ring:
For sorrow finds a swift release in song
And pride its poise.

Yet living here,
As one between two massing powers I live
whom neutrality cannot save
Nor occupation cheer.

None such shall be left alive:
The innocent wing is soon shot down,
And private stars fade in the blood-red dawn
Where two worlds strive.

The red advance of life
Contracts pride, calls out the common blood,
Beats song into a single blade,
Makes a depth-charge of grief.

Move then with new desires,
For where we used to build and love
Is no man's land, and only ghosts can live
Between two fires.

Chapter Twenty-Nine

Ralph Richardson

Ralph David Richardson was born at 11 Tivoli Road, Cheltenham on 19 December 1902 where he lived until 1907. His father had been an art teacher at Cheltenham Ladies' College. After his parents separated he lived in Sussex with his mother, working as an office boy in an insurance company. From 1917 to the mid-1920s he followed an acting career in small repertory companies, joining the Birmingham Repertory Company in 1925 where he worked with Laurence Olivier, a man a few years his junior.

From 1930 onwards he began to create a number of significant roles on the West End stage and from 1933 he became a leading figure in the Old Vic Company. The 1930s saw Richardson and Olivier establishing themselves as the two leading young Shakespearian actors on the London stage.

Ralph Richardson as Falstaff

Richardson had also begun to make a mark as a film actor and in 1936 and 1938 he starred in two of Alexander Korda's major productions, *Things to Come* (from the novel by H.G. Wells) and *South Riding* (from the novel by Winifred Holtby).

A Gloucestershire Gallery

The Opera House in Cheltenham in about 1900, now the Everyman Theatre which contains a studio theatre named after Richardson

Richardson's birthplace in Tivoli Road, Cheltenham

Together with Olivier he served in the Royal Navy during the Second World War and in 1944 Tyrone Guthrie asked them to undertake the directorship of the Old Vic which they did, with John Burrell. It was with this company that Richardson created one of his finest roles as Peer in Ibsen's *Peer Gynt*, directed by Guthrie in 1944.

By 1947 Richardson's contribution to British theatre had been recognized by the accolade of a knighthood. However, in 1948 the decision of the governors of the Old Vic to re-organize the company as part of the plan for the establishment of the National Theatre led to the resignation of all three actor/directors and one of the most fruitful partnerships in modern British theatrical history was broken up.

The company had raised the reputation of British theatre to a level of popularity and prestige that had not been seen for many years and was not to be achieved afterwards. In 1946 *The Times* had commented that Olivier and Richardson had 'once more brought the English theatre into an era of great acting'. E.G. Harcourt Williams, who had directed the Old Vic in the 1930s, was to write of their contributions that 'three men of cultural integrity and unquestioned ability in the art of theatre gathered up the threads of the original organization which the black hurricane of war had blown hither and thither and wove them into a pattern.'

Although Richardson played many important roles after this and became well known through a number of significant performances on stage, film and television his career ebbed somewhat. It was not until the middle of the 1950s that his fortunes began to revive. He avoided new plays and new authors and took a number of leading roles in classics on the stage in London and abroad. His strength had always been as a member of a repertory company and it was not until Peter Hall brought him into the National Theatre after Olivier's retirement in the 1970s that he began to play modern dress parts. His last major role was in 1982, just before his death.

His connection with Cheltenham is recognized by the Everyman Theatre where the studio theatre bears his name.

Cecil Ballantine

Chapter Thirty

Arthur Travers Harris

Arthur Travers Harris, Marshal of the RAF

Marshal of the RAF, Sir Arthur Travers Harris GCB, OBE, AFC, LLD (1892–1984) was undoubtedly one of the great air commanders of the Second World War. He had a long and distinguished military career, which culminated in his appointment as Commander-in-Chief of RAF Bomber command from February 1942 to September 1945.

Harris was born at No. 3 Queen's Parade, Cheltenham on 13 April 1892. From the age of five he was sent away to attend Gore Court School, Allhallows. After finishing his education Harris went to Rhodesia, where he tackled a variety of jobs, spending time as a tobacco planter, mail coach driver and mine worker. With the outbreak of war in 1914 he joined the 1st Rhodesian Regiment and fought briefly against the Germans in South-West Africa before transferring to the Royal Flying Corps in 1915. After gaining his wings Harris rapidly showed the qualities of a natural leader and progressed quickly through the ranks. By 1919 he was in command of No. 45 Squadron and

A Gloucestershire Gallery

The Jolly Roger, a Stirling bomber, with the air and ground crew of 199 Squadron based at North Creake airfield, Norfolk, from May 1944 to July 1945 – an example of the men Harris thought so much of

had been offered a permanent commission as a squadron leader in the newly formed Royal Air Force.

A succession of appointment in the Middle East followed, interspersed with spells at the Army Staff College, Camberley and as Commanding Officer of RAF Digby in Lincolnshire and Pembroke Dock, a flying boat base in South Wales. As the war clouds gathered in 1938 he was given the job of leading an air mission to the USA. The task of the mission was to evaluate and order suitable modern aircraft for the rapidly expanding RAF, to supplement the burgeoning production at home. The mission placed orders for 200 North American Harvard trainers and 200 twin-engined Lockheed Hudson patrol aircraft at a cost of five million pounds. Harris was promoted to Air Vice-Marshal in 1939 and became Air Officer commanding No. 5 Group, Bomber Command. During 1940–1 he was Deputy Chief of Air staff and later headed a further RAF delegation to the USA. In February 1942 he succeeded Air Marshal Sir Richard Peirse as Commander-in-Chief of Bomber Command.

3 Queen's Parade, Cheltenham, Harris' birthplace in 1892

Among his colleagues and subordinates his no nonsense attitude earned him a reputation as a hard task master, but the vast majority of those who served with and under him regarded him with the greatest respect. He was an inventive and far-sighted man who fostered the development of much in the way of new equipment and tactics, often in the face of stiff opposition from 'the men at the ministry'. He was always prepared to lend the full weight of his authority to any project that promised to enhance the efficiency of Bomber Command operations and offered his crews a better chance of survival. He is perhaps best remembered as the architect of the 'Thousand Bomber Raids' of 1942. He felt passionately that at that stage of the war the bomber force provided Britain's only means of striking back at the enemy and that the prosecution of the bomber offensive was essential for the maintenance of public morale and the will to fight on. Casualties among the bomber crews were high, some 55,000 airmen were to lose their lives, a figure that accounts for approximately 70 per cent of the total RAF casualties during the Second World War. In the face of such losses the bomber crews, with typical service cynicism, christened their chief 'Butch'. When challenged upon this subject Harris on one occasion remarked, 'You can't make omelettes without breaking eggs'. His more public nickname of 'Bomber' Harris was very much the invention of the press.

Harris retired in 1946 after being promoted Marshal of the RAF and at his own request went onto half pay. He was not feted in the way that many of his contemporaries were. Indeed in the post-war period it became fashionable to criticize the concept of the bomber offensive and Harris was often castigated by the press and others for his wartime role. He was offered a peerage by the returning Conservative government in 1951 but he declined the honour. Among his array of decorations were awards from USA, France, the Soviet Union, Brazil and Poland as well as those of his homeland. His one lasting sadness was that the airmen for whom he had such high regard were not awarded the distinction of a special medal to mark their participation in one of the most prolonged and bloody offensives of the Second World War.

Harris' birthplace is Cheltenham is marked with a plaque, which he unveiled shortly before he died.

John Rennison